How children learn

Educational theories and approaches – from Comenius the father of modern education to giants such as Piaget, Vygotsky and Malaguzzi

by Linda Pound

Contents

Published by Practical Pre-School Books, A Division of MA Education Ltd, St Jude's Church, Dulwich Road, Herne Hill, London, SE24 0PB.

Tel: 020 7738 5454 www.practicalpreschoolbooks.com

Associate Publisher: Angela Morano Shaw

© MA Education Ltd 2014. Photos on cover by Lucie Carlier

Design: Alison Cutler **fonthill**creative 01722 717043

ISBN 978-1-909280-73-1

Introduction

This book is an attempt to explain educational and psychological theories about how children learn. It provides food for thought for reflective practitioners, encouraging you to pause and reconsider why you do what you do.

Theories can be rooted in research and experimentation or they may be philosophical and hypothetical. Whatever their basis, the importance of observation is a common strand in the work of many theorists who were interested in finding out how children learn. Some were academics who became interested in children – others were experienced in working with children and developed theories to help them understand their experience. What is interesting is how often ideas which were based purely on observation are now supported by developmental theory.

We have singled out some of the key figures involved with theories about learning, particularly in the early years of education. In some cases these are linked to wider movements. Sigmund Freud, for example, is probably the best known psychoanalyst. However, other figures with psychoanalytical backgrounds who have perhaps had greater influence in education have also been included.

It is not clear why some names are remembered and others are not. Sigmund Freud is probably the best known psychoanalyst in this country, but in the United States Erikson and Fromm are more influential, perhaps because Freud fled from the Nazis to England, while Erikson and Fromm went to America.

Howard Gardner[1] says that 'great psychologists put forward complex and intricate theories, but they are often remembered best for a striking demonstration. The founding behaviourist, Ivan Pavlov, showed that dogs can be conditioned to salivate at the sound of a bell. The founding psychoanalyst, Sigmund Freud, demonstrated that unconscious wishes – for example sexual satisfaction – are reflected in ordinary dreams or slips of the tongue. And Jean Piaget (1896-1980), the most important student of intellectual development, showed that young children are not able to conserve quantities, such as liquids.' This is something to think about as you read.

About this book

- To create a sense of the way in which ideas have developed and evolved, the theorists are taken in chronological order. Where a section focuses on an individual this is according to their date of birth. This does not work in every case – Piaget and Vygotsky, for example, were contemporaries but Vygotsky's work was not widely known until some time after his death.

- Towards the end of the book you will find sections relating not to individual or groups of theorists but to broader ideas. Two of these sections relate to approaches which have no clearly identifiable leading theorist. Te Whāriki was developed in New Zealand as a government initiative, with groups of academics and practitioners including Margaret Carr and Helen May. Forest schools are widely regarded as having arisen from practice in Scandinavia but as the section on forest school shows there is a longer history. The three remaining sections focus on areas of interest to early childhood practitioners namely learning through play; research into brain development and emotional intelligence.

- Each section follows a similar format, beginning with some historical background and biographical details, where relevant, to place the person or topic in context. Significant dates are listed at the beginning of each section. The theory is explained and the titles of some of the books or articles they have written are listed. The influence that each theory has had and the criticisms which it has received are examined. Some of the specialist terms used in relation to a particular theory or topic are included in a glossary and each section includes some points for reflection to help you to apply the theory or approach to your own experience.

- There is also an attempt to link the theory with practice and to indicate what practice based on a particular theory would look

Interaction with nature was a common strand in the thinking of the early theorist

The child is at the centre of the learning process

like. Much of the practice you will see or read about has key features which appear similar. The importance of observing children is emphasised within all approaches. Outdoor experience is a common theme and the link with nature was a vital element of all the pioneer thinking about early childhood education, permeating much of the eighteenth and nineteenth century writing and thinking. In the twentieth century Margaret McMillan and Susan Isaacs did much to promote outdoor play and in the twenty-first century forest schools continue to focus on the importance of nature.

◼ You will find many other strands and connections as you read. Margaret Donaldson, for example, spent time with Piaget and Bruner. Pestalozzi was influenced by Jean-Jacques Rousseau and in turn influenced Robert Owen and Friedrich Froebel. Links with other theorists are highlighted in each section.

Overall this book can only serve as an introduction to the fascinating history and development of early childhood care and education. We hope that it will encourage you to delve deeper, helping you to understand and reflect on how you work with young children.

NOTE TO STUDENTS

Every effort has been made to make sure that you have the information you will need to cite sources in your essays and projects. You may need to rearrange these references in your written work to meet the demands of your tutors or courses. Double check before you hand in work that you have met the relevant requirements. At the end of the book you will find information relating to each section giving references and suggestions for further reading. Remember that the information in this book is by no means the end of the story. There is much more to be read and learned from the remarkable figures outlined here. Many of the books mentioned are no longer in print, so check to see if your library can get a copy. Some of these books are available in full or part text on the internet.

A word of caution about websites: some contain excellent information, others are worthless. Always think about who has published the information and why. Any website addresses provided were valid at the time of going to press.

John Comenius

PROFILE

Born in the late sixteenth century, John Comenius has been called the father of modern education. His thinking and philosophy have had a strong influence on the way in which we view learning today.

KEY DATES

1592	Born in Moravia, now part of the Czech Republic, as Jan Komensky
1638	Invited to restructure the Swedish school system
1658	Publishes one of the first illustrated books for children, *The Visible World in Pictures*
1670	Dies in Amsterdam

LINKS

Pestalozzi
Piaget

His life

Jan Amos Komensky was born in Moravia in 1592, around the same time as the scientist, Galileo, the painter, Rembrandt and the writer, Milton. These three were significant figures at the beginning of a period known as the Age of Reason when thinking was characterised by people with enquiring minds who wanted evidence for arguments and often rejected traditional religious beliefs.

Comenius – as Komensky became known in a Latinised version of his name – was educated at the University of Heidelberg before becoming a bishop in the Moravian Church. It is thought that he was approached to become the first president of Harvard University, which was established in 1636, but declined because of the Church's troubles at that time.

In 1638 he was approached to restructure the Swedish school system – a role he took up in 1642. He was also invited to become a member of an English commission for the reform of education. Although he came to England, the Civil War made progress impossible and he left

for Sweden. He died in Amsterdam in 1670 but after his death, his grandson became a bishop and presided over the renewal of the Church.

His writing

Comenius wrote more than 150 books, mostly on philosophy and theology. He wrote a novel called *The Labyrinth of the World* [1], which has been likened to John Bunyan's *Pilgrim's Progress*. In 1631, he published a book called *The Gate of Tongues Unlocked* which was designed to help children learn Latin through their first language. This was a significant shift from the normal approaches to learning Latin used at that time. He developed this approach further with the publication, in 1658, of one of the first picture books for children, *The Visible World in Pictures*. It consisted of illustrations labelled in both Latin and the child's home language. It was translated into English in 1659.

His theory

Comenius believed that education begins in early childhood and should continue throughout life. He recommended sensory experiences rather than rote learning and was in favour of formal educational opportunities for women – an unusual idea in the seventeenth century. He established a branch of philosophy that he called pansophism, which literally means 'all knowledge'. He believed that knowledge or learning, spirituality and emotional development were inseparable – a holistic view of education.

Putting the theory into practice

Comenius had high ideals and talked of developing schooling through play. There were few if any precursors to this in the seventeenth century. His emphasis on the senses was largely implemented through introducing illustrations to books. However, this was a radical step at the time. Education for girls and for the disabled were central to his belief about education. He wrote in 1657 that "the slower and weaker the disposition of any man, the more he needs assistance.... Nor can any man be found whose intellect is so weak that it cannot be improved" [2].

Of girls he wrote that "they are endowed with equal sharpness of mind and capacity for knowledge... and they are able to attain the highest positions... (in) the study of medicine and other things which benefit the human race" [2]. He also believed, perhaps uniquely at that time, that a system of education should begin with the very young. Perhaps these are the reasons that he has been referred to as the "father of modern education" [3].

What does practice look like?

After so many centuries, it is difficult to know exactly what a classroom designed by Comenius would have looked like. We do however know that although illustrated books for children and teaching in a child's first language may seem like common sense today at that time his views were considered radical and exciting. Why else would he be invited to develop education in America, Sweden, Hungary and England?

Comenius favoured inclusive practice involving everyone, and teaching that encouraged learners to use their senses. He discouraged rote learning that would have been the more usual approach in the seventeenth century.

Above all he would encourage teachers to take account both of children's developmental needs as learners as well as their individuality. Milestones and patterns of development had not been formally established at that time. In arguing for the unique needs of individual children Comenius would be relying on his own observation and insight into children's learning.

Perhaps above all, Comenius' practice was characterised by kindness. He wrote that adults should "teach gently"[3] ensuring that the experience of education was pleasurable for adults and children.

Comenius was amongst the first to devise picture books for children

Although Comenius' work was forward looking, it was a long way from what is now seen as learner-centred education. His idea of holistic education included the spiritual aspects of development and emotions but not physical development.

His influence

Comenius' theories paved the way for subsequent developments in education. To us in the twenty first century it is perhaps unthinkable that attempts would be made to teach young children in Latin but Comenius was amongst those whose work changed ideas, highlighting the importance of a child's first language. The fact that so many nations sought his advice has earnt him the title of "teacher of nations"[3]. His understanding of the importance of learning through the senses and of the holistic nature of learning remain cornerstones of educational theories today.

Piaget[4] wrote of his influence and argued that we must be careful not to jump too quickly to the idea that writing from centuries before has shaped current understanding. However, in the case of Comenius, Piaget suggests, it is difficult not to believe that later theories were built around his innovative ideas.

Common criticisms of his theory

Despite his international reputation in his lifetime, there would have been many people ready to criticise Comenius' work and philosophy. Some criticisms would have come from those holding conflicting religious views. There would also have been those who regarded the education of girls or the use of the home language as entirely unacceptable.

POINTS FOR REFLECTION

○ Why do you think physical development was not seen as part of a holistic approach to education by Comenius?

○ Try to imagine what early childhood practice would look like if it catered only for the sons of rich parents, relied on rote learning and was given in Latin without picture books. Think too about how Comenius' ideas might have been received by his contemporaries.

○ What in your view are the implications of Comenius' statement that there is no one who cannot benefit from education?

Jean-Jacques Rousseau

PROFILE

Jean-Jacques Rousseau was a Swiss philosopher whose book, *Emile*, influenced child-rearing practices in eighteenth century France. Rousseau's educational theories continued to influence theorists and philosophers throughout the eighteenth and nineteenth centuries.

KEY DATES

1712	Born in Geneva, Switzerland
1740	Becomes a tutor in Lyon
1745	Begins a relationship with Therese Levasseur
1762	*Emile* is published
1778	Dies in Ermenonville, France

LINKS

Pestalozzi
Froebel

His life

Jean-Jacques Rousseau's mother died when he was just a few days old and he was brought up by his father and an aunt. At the age of 12 he was apprenticed to an engraver who treated him badly and when he was 16 he ran away. For the next ten years he travelled, staying in France and Italy. At 18, he decided to teach music, but gave up when he found he was only a little ahead of his pupils. His attempt to tutor two small boys in Lyon in 1740 lasted less than a year. It did, however, start him thinking about education.

In 1745, Rousseau began a relationship with Therese Levasseur, who was to bear him five children. All five were placed in an orphanage soon after their birth, it is said against their mother's wishes. It is also said that Rousseau came to regret this action later.[1] Rousseau wrote a number of books, but it was one called *Emile* that earned him a name in France. Parents claimed to be bringing up their children a la Jean-Jacques – which involved not having a wet nurse, being bathed in cold water and being flimsily dressed – to be closer to nature. After his death, in 1778, crowds paid homage to him at his burial place.

His writing

Jean-Jacques Rousseau wrote a mixture of novels and non-fiction books on music, philosophy and politics. *Emile* – his book on education – is a mixture of fiction and philosophy. He also wrote a book called *The Social Contract*. (Both are published by Penguin.)

His theory

Rousseau described children as noble savages. He believed that we are born essentially good and are part of nature. Nature made children to be loved and helped but because they are innocent this help should not be intrusive. He wrote that adults should let children be children and revere childhood. He also believed in fostering self-reliance.

He suggested three broad stages of development. The first, up to 12 years of age, he saw as a stage when children were animal like. The second from 12 to 16 years of age represented the beginning of rational thought, while from 16 onwards adulthood began.

Rousseau thought that governments should work to establish freedom, equality and justice. Their role was not just to allow the will of the majority to hold sway but to take on the task of ensuring that everyone, including the weak, was protected. Education would support this process by cultivating the good in people. We should all be educated for our own good, not for that of society which, Rousseau said, was corrupt.

Putting the theory into practice

Rousseau never put his theories into practice – indeed he sent his own children to live in orphanages. However, many parents in eighteenth century France were influenced by Rousseau's writing. Until then, among members of French society it was accepted practice to place babies with wet nurses and swaddle them for their early months. This changed and the changes were largely attributed to Rousseau. Other writers and thinkers condemned some of the practices adopted.

Rousseau believed in freedom. He wrote, for example[1] that 'the only habit the child should be allowed is that of having no habits... Reverse the usual procedure and you will almost always do right'. Freedom (for boys) was to involve integration with nature. Development was driven by nature and, in his view, contact with society corrupted children. This is reflected in his famous words written in 1762[2] that "Man is born free but everywhere he is in chains". Emile, the subject of Rousseau's

Freedom involved integration with nature

famous book of the same name, is depicted as growing up in the countryside where nature provided his education and taught him how to live in freedom.

His influence

Rousseau's immediate influence on eighteenth century Paris may not have been what he wished but over time, it can be seen that his influence has been great. While many of Rousseau's theories appear far-fetched, he enabled people to think differently about the way in which children should be educated. His overwhelming contribution to education has more to do with freeing up thinking, encouraging people to consider and try new ideas. In 1788, after Rousseau's death, Madame de Stael, an eighteenth century writer and society figure, claimed that he 'had succeeded in restoring happiness to childhood'.[1]

His emphasis on the role of nature in education has had a very long-term influence, beginning with the work of Pestalozzi, who in turn influenced Froebel. We might say that this focus continues to influence thinking about the education of young children through forest schools and through the overall emphasis on the importance, for both physical and emotional well-being, of outdoor play.

In highlighting the importance of observation, Rousseau has influenced the development of early childhood education. In advocating that teachers take time to notice what and how children are learning he helped to shift the focus of education away from what was being taught to what was being learnt.

Common criticisms of his theory

The definitions which Rousseau uses in his writing make it difficult to follow exactly what he means. He says repeatedly, for example, that 'the first impulses of nature are always right'.[1] However, he supports this claim by asserting that behaviour that is not inherently good cannot be natural. By this reasoning, any bad or evil actions are not part of nature.

What does practice look like?

It is difficult to say what practice would have looked like since as Rousseau himself stated he was, in his writing, presenting "an ideal, not a reality; a philosophical position rather than a "true treatise on education""[2]. He emphasised freedom and kindness, opportunities to be at liberty amongst woods and flowers, growing up in a natural environment. However, his ideas were often put into practice in ways which appear neglectful. In a description of the children of Paris, who were apparently being raised 'a la Jean-Jacques'[1], we see that while freedom included freedom from the swaddling clothes which restricted movement in infancy, it was also sometimes interpreted as letting children run about in light clothing even in bitter winter weather. There were moreover critics who claimed that in too many children 'hair straggles in a hideous and disgusting way... They are no longer checked but clamber on to you with their muddy feet. When you visit their parents they deafen you with their noise, and just when their father or mother is about to reply to you on some important matter, you see them choose instead to answer some childish question of their darling son or daughter..... It is Emile which is responsible for this provoking, obstinate, insolent, impudent, arrogant generation'.[1]

The role of the teacher was primarily to observe. He said that teachers should 'take time to observe nature; watch your scholar well before you say a word to him; first leave the germ of his character free to show itself.'[1] He even suggested that teachers 'must know how to waste time in order to save it'[2] – indicating a preference for a relaxed, carefree learning environment.

His belief in the importance of freedom is supported by arguing that if a person does not feel constrained, then their liberty is not infringed. For Rousseau, 'Man feels free when he wants only what is within his reach'.[1] In other words, self-discipline is the only true freedom. The main criticism of his work is that his ideas were not practical and were open to misinterpretation.

Rousseau has also been criticised for the fact that his philosophy was to be applied only to boys. For girls, obedience was considered to be of prime importance.

"Watch your scholar well before you say a word to him."

GLOSSARY

A la Jean-Jacques: a phrase used to describe an upbringing in what was believed to be the style advocated by Rousseau with an emphasis on freedom and nature

POINTS FOR REFLECTION

○ Rousseau's work highlights the difficulties of an emphasis on liberty. Do you agree that self-discipline is the only true freedom? What do you think it means in educational terms?

○ Rousseau emphasised observation as a means of understanding children's nature. Think of some examples of observations which have helped you to understand their nature or characteristics. What do you think is meant by the idea that adults must waste time in order to save it?

Johann Pestalozzi

PROFILE

Pestalozzi was a Swiss educator whose ideas and practices laid the foundation for the reform of nineteenth century education. He put forward radical ideas that were later taken up and have now been absorbed into the way we educate young children.

KEY DATES

1746	Born in Zurich, Switzerland
1770	Birth of son, named Jean-Jacques after Rousseau
1773	Opens experimental school
1799	Takes in war orphans at a school in Stans
1800	Directs educational establishment at Burgdorf
1801	*How Gertrude Teaches her Children*, the best known of Pestalozzi's books, is published
1805	Opens Yverdun Institute
1808	Works with Froebel
1818	Owen visits Yverdun
1827	Dies

LINKS

Comenius
Rousseau
Owen
Froebel

Children "should be taught by nature"

His life

Johann Heinrich Pestalozzi was born in Zurich, Switzerland in 1746, the second of three surviving children. His father, a surgeon, died when Pestalozzi was five, leaving his mother to bring them up with the help of the family servant. Reports of his childhood differ – some claiming a happy childhood; others that his childhood was severely restricted – not allowed out to play and rarely joined by other children. Johann went to school and learned easily, though he was often thought of as socially inept and teased by other children. His philosophy later in life was to value idiosyncracies as "the greatest blessing of nature".

During his childhood, Pestalozzi would visit his grandfather at Höngg, and there he became interested in the differences between country and townspeople. These experiences, together with the loyalty and devotion shown by his family's servant, developed his respect for the poor. He thought that children in the country seemed contented. He also noticed that once they started school it seemed as though they lost their vitality. These insights were to influence his later theories and practice.

Pestalozzi undertook some study but grew tired of academic life and decided to study farming. He met and fell in love with Anna Schulthess, and bought a house and some neglected land at Neuhof near the River Aare. In 1769 he married Anna. In 1770, Pestalozzi and his wife had a son, Jean-Jacques, named after Jean-Jacques Rousseau. He was a sickly child. Pestalozzi's wife became seriously ill and the family was virtually destitute. Pestalozzi became a laughing stock in the town for his failures.

Five years later his farming enterprise failed but he remained interested in the poor and helping the wider community and began taking children into his home. He taught them spinning, weaving, sewing and cooking. The idea was to teach the children to become self-supporting but this enterprise too failed. Eventually, after a further five years, the children were sent away. Despite all, Pestalozzi continued to believe that his ideas for the education of the poor were practical and well-founded.

Children were encouraged to observe nature

After the French Revolution, Pestalozzi sought and gained government approval to set up a school in Stans for war orphans. He cared for them almost single-handedly and tried to restore their lives. He later said that these exhausting months in 1799 were the happiest of his life. At first there were 50 children but the numbers grew to 80. Pestalozzi commented on the scabies, open sores, ragged clothing, and overall physical plight of these children. Within five months, they were living together happily.

But the project took its toll on Pestalozzi's health and the school closed. Another was established in Burgdorf, where he stayed for a number of years but never lost the ambition to set up an industrial school for poor children. These years were invaluable in enabling Pestalozzi to formulate his educational theories.

But again Pestalozzi's grand plans failed and the institute closed. During its last year he wrote his great political work, *To the Innocence, the Earnestness and the Generosity of My Age and My Country*. Towards the end of his life, Pestalozzi wrote constantly about his ideas and theories. He died in 1827.

His writing

In 1780, Pestalozzi started writing, setting out his theories of education. One of his most famous works, *Leonard and Gertrude*, was an instant success. It was the first realistic representation of rural life in that part of Europe. It told the story of a woman who exposed corruption and, by her well-ordered home, set a model for the village school and wider community.

For 30 years, Pestalozzi lived in virtual isolation writing about education, politics and economics. His most influential book remained *How Gertrude Teaches her Children*. It was about education and was published in 1801.

His theory

It has been suggested that Pestalozzi 'may fairly be regarded as the starting point of modern educational theory and practice'[1]. He believed, like Jean-Jacques Rousseau, that education must be

How children learn

'according to nature'. For Pestalozzi, however, security in the home was the foundation of happiness and, since it formed the basis of children's reality, was also the foundation for learning. Like Comenius, he believed that all children had an equal right to education and the capacity to profit from it. He attacked conventional education for being dull and too little concerned with interest and experience. Like Rousseau, he thought that children's innate faculties should be developed in accordance with nature. Children should be given real experiences and encouraged to engage with real things. Progress from the familiar to the new should be in a loving and secure environment.

Pestalozzi emphasised the unique nature of the individual and the inner dignity of everyone. He believed that every child has potential but that without love neither physical nor intellectual powers can develop naturally. He wrote that love, work and social interaction were the foundations of development.

Putting the theory into practice

Emphasising the importance of social interaction, Pestalozzi thought that children should be taught in groups according to their ability, not necessarily their age. The practical elements of his work owe something to Comenius (see pages 4-5) in that he emphasised the importance of the senses and based learning on the familiar. Spelling and reading were practised with moveable letters, pebbles and beans, and even apples and cakes were used for sums and fractions. Only when mathematical ideas were fully understood, did Pestalozzi teach children numbers. This was a far cry from the conventional education of the early 1800s but very much in line with current thinking.

For Pestalozzi the most important sensory experience was observation. He led what were known as 'object lessons' and linked these to actions since, for him, action must follow perception. He argued that life shapes us and the life that shapes us is not a matter of words but actions – education involves the repetition of actions. He further suggested that schooling should not be about blind obedience or diligence in set tasks but in "interdependent action and fitness for life"[2].

His influence

Friedrich Froebel (see pages 17-20) and Robert Owen (see pages 13-16) both spent time at Yverdun. Froebel in particular was heavily influenced by Pestalozzi's work. Both Owen and Froebel built on the link between childhood and the natural world, Rousseau's focus which was enhanced and made practical by Pestalozzi. Many of the phrases today associated with Froebel (such as 'learning by doing' and 'making the inner outer') were taken from Pestalozzi. Owen had some criticisms of Yverdun, yet he sent some of his sons to a school which had been set up by one of Pestalozzi's followers because he admired the belief that rich and poor should be educated in similar ways.

The tradition established by Pestalozzi and his wife of taking in underprivileged children has been perpetuated in the Pestalozzi

What does practice look like?

In 1805 Pestalozzi opened a boarding school at Yverdun which became world famous and drew pupils from all over Europe. The school relied on fee-paying pupils but some poor children were taken in to satisfy Pestalozzi's lifelong wish to educate the poor. It had up to 250 pupils at any one time. His approach to education not only aimed to involve all classes, Pestalozzi also believed that girls should be educated together with boys. Children were given plenty of exercise in the fresh air, nourishing food, had ten lessons a day (starting at six in the morning), enjoyed swimming, tobogganing and long walks.

The institute attracted the attention of Friedrich Froebel (see pages 17-20) because of its emphasis on outdoor pursuits such as gardening. Robert Owen (see pages 13-16) visited Yverdun and for him the attraction was the school's focus on educating rich and poor together. He was also attracted by the school's focus on developing children's ability to live independently – through growing food, and learning manual skills.

Pestalozzi's approach had two parts – a general method and a special method[3]. The general focused on the importance of a secure and loving environment while the special emphasised the importance of learning through first-hand experience and observation. Pestalozzi wrote in his diary[4] that children should be "taught by nature rather than by you... should a bird sing or an insect hum on a leaf, at once stop your walk; bird and insect are teaching him; you may be silent."

Education was based on the natural world

Children's Villages. At the end of the Second World War, the Swiss humanist, Dr Walter Corti (1910-90), wanted to help orphaned and refugee children. He set up a village at Trogen in Switzerland in Pestalozzi's name. In 1957, a second Pestalozzi village was established in East Sussex, UK. Originally, the English school took children from the age of nine whose lives had been devastated by war. Then it helped children from other conflicts, before including Third World countries. Today there is worldwide work in a range of Pestalozzi Children's Villages.

Today his influence may be found in the emphasis on outdoor education. Like Comenius and Rousseau before him, his emphasis on the observation of children continues to be seen as a vital element of successful practice. The importance of a secure and loving environment which promotes social interaction is also an important legacy.

It is for these reasons that Pestalozzi is widely described as having created the starting point for modern educational practice.

Common criticisms of his theory

Pestalozzi was not generally regarded as successful. The schools he established were not open for long. Owen believed that Yverdun was less successful than his school in New Lanark at providing children with life skills. Perhaps Pestalozzi's dream of providing a practical education fell down because he was not entirely practical himself (though certainly more practical than Rousseau that he so much admired). Although he built on many of Pestalozzi's theories, Froebel

believed that Pestalozzi did not pay enough attention to physical involvement in learning. His occupations and activities were designed to address what he saw as a flaw in Pestalozzi's work.

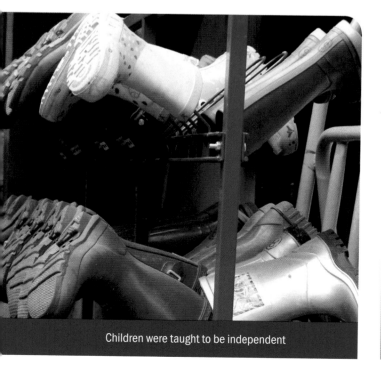
Children were taught to be independent

POINTS FOR REFLECTION

○ Do you agree that education should focus on fitness for life? What do you do in your setting that supports this view?

○ Pestalozzi appears to put more emphasis on children looking at things rather than handling them. Why do you think this might be? Are there any advantages?

○ What elements of your practice aim to promote social interaction?

Robert Owen

PROFILE

Robert Owen, a self-made Welsh businessman and internationally renowned philanthropist, set up the first workplace nursery in Britain at his cotton mills in New Lanark in Scotland. Many of his policies and ideas about communities and education were ahead of their time.

KEY DATES

1771	Born in Newtown, Wales
1815	Establishes factory in New Lanark
1816	New Lanark infant school opens, catering for children aged two to six
1818	Visits Pestalozzi at Yverdun
1825	Establishes New Harmony village in USA
1858	Dies in Newtown, his birthplace

LINKS

Pestalozzi

His life

By the age of 7, Robert Owen had become a pupil-teacher and by the age of 9 had left school to work as a grocery boy. He subsequently worked in a saddler and as a postmaster. Having married the daughter of a mill-owner, in 1815, Robert Owen set up a new factory complex where cotton was manufactured in New Lanark in Scotland. Many of his workers were destitute refugees, evicted from the land clearance in the Highlands of Scotland. Owen believed he should provide for their welfare and built housing, social facilities and a school. He recognised the childcare problems which women workers faced and provided a nursery, known at that time as an infant school.

Owen was a businessman. He claimed that by catering for the needs of families and children his manufacturing profits rose. The workforce was happy and therefore productive. His focus on young children also promised continuing profitability. He also sought to engineer social change, hoping to replace the competitive and class-bound society of that period with one which was more socialist in outlook. Owen was

opposed to child labour and the provision made for children at New Lanark had some influence in changing opinions. Although neither employers nor government showed much concern for the welfare of workers, Owen was instrumental in changing the law on child labour.

In 1825, Robert Owen went to America for a short time. He had bought a village and created a venture that he called New Harmony. His aim was to establish a 'community of equality' where people lived communally, ate together in the same place and wore similar clothes. Owen never lived there but some of his children did. The constitution included objectives[1] which emphasised the importance of equality and freedom, including:

- equality of rights, uninfluenced by sex or condition, in all adults;
- equality of duties, modified by physical and mental conformation;
- co-operative union, in the business and amusements of life;
- community of property;
- freedom of speech and action;
- sincerity in all our proceedings;

Singing and dancing were encouraged

Owen believed that knowledge of geography would broaden children's horizons

- kindness in all our actions;

- courtesy in all our intercourse;

- order in all our arrangements;

- preservation of health;

- acquisition of knowledge;

- the practice of economy, or of producing and using the best of everything in the most beneficial manner;

- obedience to the laws of the country in which we live.

In both New Lanark and New Harmony radical ideas on the environment, concern for social well-being and a sense of community were seen as being connected to the education not just of young children but of adults as well. These ideas, still seen as aspirational today, must have seemed revolutionary during Owen's lifetime.

His writing

Robert Owen wrote a vast number of political pamphlets and books. The website of the Robert Owen museum in Newtown, his birthplace, indicates that he wrote more than thirty publications. It identifies *A New View of Society* (published in 1812) as his major work. It also has his plan for the permanent relief of the working classes, which was published on behalf of the British and Foreign Philanthropic Society, 10 years later in 1822. In this he identifies the advantages for the poor of working in a rural mill such as he set up in New Lanark. He contrasts these with the fate of those living and working in the wretched towns and cities that had mushroomed as a result of the Industrial Revolution. In 1836 he published his autobiography which was entitled *The New Moral World*.

His theory

Owen believed that the experiences we offer young children have a lifelong impact on the way in which they develop. Two statements are important in understanding Robert Owen's educational theories[2].

They are:

'Man is a compound being, whose character is formed of his constitution or organisation at birth, and of the effects of external circumstances acting upon that organisation, which effects continue to operate upon and to influence him from birth to death...' and

'Nevertheless, the constitution of every infant, except in the case of organic disease, is capable of being formed or nurtured, either into a very inferior or a very superior being, according to the qualities of the external circumstances allowed to influence that constitution from birth.'

These statements demonstrate that unlike some earlier (and subsequent) theorists, Owen believed that children were shaped by both their genetic inheritance and by their lifelong experiences. To understand his theory it is necessary to understand that Owen was out of step with almost all of his contemporaries. Owen was a social reformer who lived by his own beliefs. In sending some of his sons to a school run by a follower of Pestalozzi he demonstrated his commitment to the education of rich and poor in a similar way. He rejected religion apparently stating that "there is something wrong with all religions".[3]

In developing his theory Owen visited a number of experimental schools in Europe, including Pestalozzi's school at Yverdun. The two men shared a belief in the importance of early education, of sensory experience and of the environment – although Owen is reported to have believed that New Lanark was better at ensuring that children had the skills with which to earn a living and at nurturing positive dispositions for learning [1].

Where Owen was in step with other radical thinkers of his time was in a growing belief, reflected in the ideas of Romantics such as Rousseau, that childhood was of great importance in shaping the child's future and that childhood should be a happy time. If childhood innocence could be protected by adults, then Owen and others believed, there was hope for the future. Owen's theory therefore was that if the children of the working class could be protected and given a decent life during childhood, then their future would be assured.

Putting the theory into practice

In order to put his theory into practice, Owen created at New Lanark a manufacturing environment which gave workers a decent environment. He paid better than average wages, provided housing and education for all, including working adults. Even more unusually, the school at New Lanark was an early attempt to provide group care and education for the very young children of working class parents, and is sometimes described as the first workplace nursery.

The principles underpinning practice included:

- a focus on geography. Owen's socialist views encouraged him to look beyond Britain's shores to Europe and beyond. In addition to

What does practice look like?

His expectation was that this kindness would be imitated and that children would be kind to one another. His reminders to staff to show 'unceasing kindness, in tone, look, word and action, to all the children without exception'[2] reflect his genuine liking for children.

The schoolroom at New Lanark has been described[2] as being 'furnished with paintings, chiefly of animals, with maps, and often supplied with natural objects from the garden, fields and woods – the examination and explanation of which always excited their curiosity and created an animated conversation between the children and their instructors'.

He provided musicians and hired artists to paint murals. He even bought a baby alligator to stimulate interest in natural history and geography. Children stayed at school until the age of ten but classes were also provided for adults.

Children were encouraged to spend many hours each day in the open air and there was a strong emphasis on physical activity and music – singing, marching to music, fife playing and dancing. Dancing lessons began at the age of two and children became highly competent at, what a contemporary writer described as 'all the dances of Europe'. This was said to be because Robert Owen had 'discovered that dancing is one means of reforming vicious habits... by promoting cheerfulness and contentment... thus diverting attention from things that are vile and degrading'[1]. Books were considered inappropriate for young children. Geography had a 'strong moral undertone, for the children were often reminded that but for an accident of birth they might have been born into a different society with values totally unlike those of their own'[1]. The emphasis was on morality, on respecting others and never acting in unkind ways.

the settlement in New Harmony, he argued for the establishment of new towns as far afield as Australia. Geography would broaden children's horizons;

- a focus on equality. Although morality was very much part of a Victorian education, for Owen, this must include equality;

- fun, excitement, conversation and well-being. For Owen all these elements contributed to the happy childhood he sought for all children;

- physical well-being through outdoor provision, exercise, fresh air and nourishment.

His influence

Robert Owen has been described as 'one of the most important and controversial figures of his generation'[10]. Moreover he has also been described as one of the first modern educators whose ideas about the treatment of those in poverty can be seen reflected in current ideas about a need for universal early years provision. The ideas that Owen developed in New Lanark were highly influential in changing attitudes about child labour. He was to be instrumental in changing employment law (Factory Act 1819) so that children under 10 could no longer work. The law also reduced working hours for children over ten years of age.

His commitment to education, not just for children but as a lifelong process, was also radical, as were his ideas about the importance of equality. It was his ideas that led to the formation of the Co-operative movement. His work is widely recognised in China.

The New Lanark nursery attracted many visitors and although it did not have much impact on provision for young children in England, it was influential in Scotland. In Glasgow, close to New Lanark, two similar schools (known at that time as infant schools and catering for children up to six years of age were established. These have been said to have introduced the idea of free play before Froebel[2]. The idea of combined nursery centres – offering both care and education – was taken up elsewhere in Europe (for example, the écoles maternelles which began in France in 1848) but sadly was not as well received in Britain.

Common criticisms of his theory

Education in England followed a more formal route. While government seemed anxious to get children into school early to prepare them for the world of work, Owen believed that the best preparation for the future was the development of respect, equality and cooperation. He has been described as "a lonely voice in an England convulsed with a search for power and quick wealth"[4]. It may be that his ideas came too soon, that they were simply too radical for most people.

Robert Owen's work has been criticised as being rooted in his desire for profit rather than genuine concern for the welfare of his workers and their families. However, his policies were a bold step forward and although he clearly had a good head for business it seems likely that in the climate of opinion at that time his basic motive was equality and fairness.

Owen has been criticised for admitting children from as young as one year of age to his nursery. Was it concern for children – or was it motivated by commercial profit? Or was it seen as an opportunity to get mothers back to work sooner? This area of criticism has been linked to an idea which has dogged nursery education. Van der Eyken writing in the 1960s argues that nursery education became associated with rescuing the poor from a life that is 'vile and degrading'[1] that "it has made harder the task of convincing society as a whole that the early years of any child are too important to be left unattended"[4]. In other words nursery education was seen as only necessary for the children of the poor – not needed by more advantaged families. It seems unlikely given Owen's commitment to the integration of poor and rich and his concern for others that this was his view – merely the way in which it became interpreted by others.

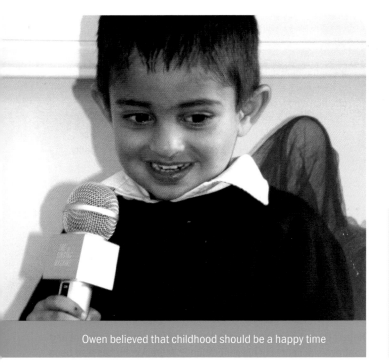

Owen believed that childhood should be a happy time

POINTS FOR REFLECTION

○ Do you agree that happiness is important in early childhood? Give your reasons.

○ Do you agree that singing and dancing are important? Give your reasons.

○ Why is nursery education important for all children – not just the poor?

Friedrich Froebel

PROFILE

Friedrich Froebel is widely associated with his words "play is a child's work". He saw childhood as part of nature, a time of life steeped in spirituality. His influence is seen today in the emphasis on play and outdoor provision in early childhood education. He is also credited with having pioneered child-centred approaches to learning.

KEY DATES

1782	Born in Thuringia, Prussia (now Germany)
1808	Teaches at Pestalozzi's school in Switzerland
1816	Sets up own school in Griesheim
1818	Sets up school in Keilhau
1826	*The Education of Man* is published
1852	Dies
1854	Beginning of Froebelian training in England
1857	Froebelian training courses certificated by the Froebel Society for the Promotion of the Kindergarten System

LINKS

Rousseau
Pestalozzi
McMillan
Athey

The garden was a vital aspect of provision

His life

Friedrich Froebel was born in 1782 in Thuringia, now part of Germany. He was the son of a clergyman and the youngest of five children. His mother died when he was nine months old. When he was ten, he went to live with an uncle who took an interest in him and sent him to school. He enjoyed mathematics and languages but his great passion was nature, particularly plants.

After leaving school he became an apprentice forester. After two years he took some informal courses at Jena University where he developed an appetite for philosophy and a love of intellectual learning. He read widely and studied hard and was influenced by the thinkers of the day. He took a variety of jobs, including land surveyor, estate manager and secretary until his reading led him to an interest in teaching. He spent some time teaching at Pestalozzi's school in Yverdun. Froebel went to Frankfurt to study architecture but took up teaching after meeting Anton Gruner. Gruner ran what was seen as a progressive school in Frankfurt and he gave Froebel a job there.

After further study (interrupted in 1813 by military service during the Napoleonic Wars) at the University of Gottingen, Froebel set up his own school in Griesheim in Thuringia. He was 34. In 1818, he moved the school to Keilhau in Prussia and began to put his educational theories into practice. Influenced by both Rousseau and Pestalozzi, Froebel believed in child-centred education. He and the families friends with whom he set up the school established an educational community. This is reflected in his writings when he says 'Let us live with our children, let them live with us, so we shall gain through them what all of us need'[1]. The school flourished.

At the request of the Swiss government he spent some time training teachers in Switzerland, and began work as head of a new orphanage school there. It was this job that sparked his deep interest in the early years.

Froebel died in 1852. Two years later, The Times and other respected publications published articles about his work and theories.

Wooden blocks were developed by Froebel

His writing

Froebel wrote many articles on education, but his writing does not make for easy reading. His most famous work, *The Education of Man*, was published in 1826. His style was deeply philosophical, reflecting his spiritual and religious beliefs, including his view of the unity of God, man and nature. Among the best known of his books is *Mother Play and Nursery Songs*, a book which reflected his deeply held belief in the importance of mother and child interactions.

His theory

Froebel had firm views on play and its place in child development, believing that it fostered enjoyment, emotional well-being and was a fundamental source of benefit. He insisted that the education of young children was vital to their development as individuals and to social reform. His first kindergarten was called the Child Nurture and Activity Institute. The word kindergarten can be translated either as a garden for children or a garden of children. Some writers suggest

that it refers to a garden for growing or nurturing children, while others suggest that for Froebel it carried the notion of a paradise garden. Froebel wanted the kindergarten to be an institution for the 'cultivation of family life, and the forming of national life and even of all humanity'[2].

Froebel was the first person to articulate a comprehensive theory on how children learn and give detailed instructions for putting it into practice[3]. His work gave rise to the idea of having a philosophy of education[4]. His philosophy was founded on the importance of the garden and included notions of mutual respect. This is reflected in his phrase 'at every stage be that stage' – highlighting the idea that children should be allowed to be children, enjoying the things that children enjoy without having to be concerned for what comes next. Froebel also encouraged teachers to 'begin where the learner is'.

He was fascinated by child development and would watch his friends' children play. His observations led him to reflect on the interactions between mothers and babies. He also emphasised the role of the mother in learning and believed that parents should be closely involved in their children's development and education. Froebel believed that teachers should not teach by rote, as was common at that time, but encourage self-expression through play. As Froebel became more experienced his theory developed and he came to see play as fundamental to children's development and the most spiritual or highest form of activity in which humans (not just children) engage.

He was passionate about the interconnectedness of life, beauty and knowledge. These three forms (as he called them) were connected to aspects of kindergarten provision and included sensory and first-hand experience, nature, music and the arts and mathematics. Spirituality was to be found in everything. He is described as a pantheist and therefore linked everything to God – seeing the divine in every aspect of life.

Putting the theory into practice

Froebel's theory and practice was consciously built on the work of Rousseau and Pestalozzi. All believed that the quality of the environment in which children were raised was important. There were however important differences. Froebel thought of education as a science and sought to:

- make clearer connections between subjects;

- place greater emphasis on learning by doing, rather than simply through observation and the senses;

- draw out intellectual and spiritual benefit from outdoor provision, as well as physical;

- develop the use of manufactured, structured resources alongside the use of natural materials;

- highlight the role of adults in guiding children's learning, rather than as Rousseau proposed, leaving it to nature.

Froebel stressed the fundamental role of women in the education of young children. He deliberately recruited women teachers at a time when teaching was largely seen as a male role. This owed much to the deprivation that Froebel believed he had suffered because of his own mother's death. He wrote that the death of his mother influenced his whole future development and described the misery of his early years without a mother.

His emphasis on learning by doing was in contrast to the formal teaching common at that period. He was also among the first educationists to see the value of the sounds produced by different materials or by singing. He saw them as a means of creative expression. He developed songs and rhymes for young children, which he called 'Mother Songs'. These were published in 1878. Froebel also encouraged expressive dance which reflected the technology of his age – namely machines.

What does practice look like?

Play and the outdoor environment were, unsurprisingly, of fundamental importance in a Froebelian kindergarten. Children between the age of one and seven would be encouraged to garden and to enjoy nature and the outdoors. Nature walks were part of the provision and space and light were seen as essential to learning. Natural or elemental materials – clay, sand and water were seen as being gifts from God to meet children's learning needs. The freedom offered by these activities was to be balanced by what he termed Gifts and Occupations. We would not consider many of these activities as playful but at that time Froebel saw them as a form of play.

The Occupations included weaving, paper folding, cutting and sewing on perforated cards. Froebel developed graduated exercises which he based on the games he had observed children playing. He promoted the use of soft clay, wet sand, pieces of wood, and drawing with crayons and chalk.

The Gifts consisted of a set of playthings or structured materials. They were presented in a highly structured way. Children had to take the Gift carefully from the box and every block within the Gift had to be used and any new construction made by transforming the existing one, rather than knocking it down and starting again[5]. A special table was provided, marked in one-inch squares to encourage careful and symmetrical working. When they had finished, children had to replace the blocks in the box.

In his early writing Froebel discussed the use of large sets of blocks (around 500 in all) but in later writings he instead emphasises the Gifts which were:

Gift 1 – A box of six small soft woollen balls or spheres
Gift 2 – A wooden cube, cylinder and sphere
Gift 3 – A two-inch cube divided into eight one-inch wooden cubes
Gifts 4-6 – Each of these was cut from an eight-inch cube which was divided in different ways, into cubes, half cubes, cuboids, triangles and prisms.

Singing games were also a significant element of Froebelian practice. Froebel, who valued music at all stages of early childhood, believed that ring games strengthened social interaction – a vital element of education in the early years.

His influence

In 1857, following Froebel's death, the Froebel Society for the Promotion of the Kindergarten System began to certificate courses to ensure uniformity of standards, publicise Froebelian methods and provide teacher training to staff in kindergartens. The Froebel Educational Institute for training teachers opened in West Kensington, London, in 1894. This later moved to the present site in Roehampton, where the Froebel Institute (together with its Early Childhood Archive

Centre) forms part of Roehampton University to this day. Froebel's work attracted a lot of interest in North America and Europe where large numbers of Froebelian kindergartens opened.

Froebel's work continued to have a strong influence well into the twentieth century, even though Froebelian practice was rarely seen. A notable exception to this is the work of Margaret McMillan (see page 31) who in the final years of the nineteenth century joined the Froebel Society and used Froebelian approaches in her practice. The progressive ideals of education which grew in the years between the two world wars were firmly rooted in the philosophy which he had developed. Froebel commented on the first smile as a social action depending not only on the child's development as an individual but on the encouragement of the mother. Although, like the role of music in neonatal development, now widely accepted, this view was neither understood nor accepted in the nineteenth century.

Wooden blocks used in most early years settings are commonly assumed to have been developed by Froebel. Some writers, however, suggest that the Owenite schools established in Glasgow in the 1820s used blocks before they were included in Froebelian practice. Perhaps the fact that the latter enjoyed far more world-wide renown that Owenite practice suggests that Froebel can continue to take credit for their continued widespread use.

The Froebel Society continues to educate the public on all matters concerning young children. The Froebel Block Play project and Chris Athey's project (see page 67), for example, were funded through the society and have made a major contribution to our understanding of young children.

Gifts and Occupations were devised to develop normal dexterity

Common criticisms of his theory

Froebel's methods were often misunderstood in this country, perhaps because his work was not translated into English until 1885. The relationship between play and the use of the Gifts and the principles that underpinned them were not always clear. There was a sharp divide between what Froebel said and the intricate instructions that went with the Gifts which made the theory difficult to put into practice. Many of the Gifts and Occupations require high levels of fine motor skills but despite Froebel's emphasis on nature walks, gardening and outdoor play, his work is sometimes criticised for not focusing more on gross motor development.

Froebel recruited women and, it has been suggested, came to overstate the importance of women as teachers of young children. Although middle class in origin, Froebel's methods were adapted for use with disadvantaged children and families as nursery and infant schools were established at the beginning of the twentieth century. Some contemporary writers saw Froebel's theory as having universal application, but others felt that it did not really address the needs of poor children.

GLOSSARY

Gifts: the gifts are intended to give the child new universal aspects of the external world, suited to a child's development. The gifts lead to discovery and give insight. (For further information see http://www.froebelweb.org/web7010.html)

Kindergarten: a German word which may be interpreted to mean a garden for children; a garden of children; a garden for growing or nurturing children, or a paradise garden.

Occupations: the occupations furnish material for practice in certain skills, they lead to invention and give the child power. They involve solids (such as clay and wood); surfaces (such as paper and paint); lines (such as drawing and embroidery); points (such as bead threading) and reconstruction (such as sticks or straws). (For further information see http://www.froebelweb.org/web7010.html)

Pantheism: a set of beliefs which identifies God with the universe, or regards the universe as a manifestation of God.

POINTS FOR REFLECTION

○ From the settings you know, try to identify elements of practice which you think may have their roots in Froebelian ideas.

○ What role does music play in interactions between mothers and babies?

○ Is there a balance in your practice between fine and gross motor skills and between adult-led and child-initiated activity?

Sigmund Freud and psychoanalytic theories

PROFILE

Sigmund Freud was a neurologist who became known as the founding father of psychoanalysis. His ideas have generally been more influential in therapy than in education. However, his theories and those that derived from them are highly relevant to the care and education of young children.

KEY DATES

1856-1939	Sigmund Freud (Moravia, now part of the Czech Republic)
1875-1961	Carl Jung (Switzerland)
1882-1960	Melanie Klein (Austria)
1895-1982	Anna Freud, Sigmund Freud's youngest daughter (Austria)
1896-1971	Donald Winnicott (England)
1900-1980	Erich Fromm (Germany)
1902-1994	Erik Erikson (Germany)
1903-1990	Bruno Bettelheim (Austria)
1913	Founding of London (later British) Psychoanalytical Society

LINKS

Isaacs
Bowlby
Montessori
Piaget
Goleman

Freud emphasised the importance of emotions

His life

Sigmund Freud was born in Moravia (which was then part of Austria but is now part of the Czech Republic) in 1856, one of eight children. He began his studies in Vienna at the age of seventeen. Although he had intended to study law, he studied philosophy, physiology and zoology. In 1881 he qualified as a doctor and although he worked in a number of different hospital departments he began to specialise in neuropathology. In 1885 he went to Paris to study the work of the neurologist Charcot. Although initially interested in Charcot's use of hypnosis, Freud rapidly became much more interested in his use of free association and treatment of hysteria.

Returning to Vienna, Freud developed a theory of psychoanalysis which was to have enormous ramifications. Freud was Jewish and after the rise of the Nazi Party in Austria, he fled with his wife and children to England in 1938. Freud died shortly after, in London in 1939. His daughter Anna, youngest of six children, continued to practise in London.

Freud's lifetime saw the beginnings of psychology. In the 1870s two very influential Europeans, von Helmholtz and Wundt, began to experiment with the workings of the mind and it was undoubtedly in this climate that Freud's interest in psychoanalysis developed. He was not primarily interested in work with children, although his daughter Anna, was to

Carl Jung believed in the impact of personal and social unconsciousness on thinking and behaviour

become a foremost figure in that field. However, his work has greatly influenced both a wide range of theorists and work with young children.

The writings of psychoanalytic theorists

Freud was an immensely prolific writer. His writings have been compiled into twenty four volumes[1] but in the main do not highlight the emotional development of young children. However, many of the psychotherapeutic writers who followed him did focus on children. The books listed below have been selected from a number of different theorists as being particularly relevant:

- *Psycho-Analytic Treatment of Children, Part 1*, Anna Freud (1926)

- *A Symposium on Child Analysis*, Melanie Klein (1927)

- *Psycho-Analytic Treatment of Children, Part 2*, Anna Freud (1927)

- *Childhood and Society*, Erik Erikson (1950)

- *The Child, the Family and the Outside World*, Donald Winnicott (1957)

- *Playing and Reality*, Donald Winnicott (1971)

- *The Piggle: an account of the psycho-analytic treatment of a little girl*, Donald Winnicott (1977)

- *The Uses of Enchantment: The Meaning and Importance of Fairy Tales*, Bruno Bettelheim (1976)

His theory

Psychoanalysis can be defined as a means of helping patients to deal with emotional problems or disorders by probing unconscious thought. Sigmund Freud described it as 'the talking cure'. The term psychoanalysis is most closely applied to Freud's own work while psychodynamics is a more general term for therapies (including psychoanalysis) designed to explore the psychological forces that shape behaviour and emotions. The relationship between conscious and unconscious decisions and actions is of particular interest as is the impact of our experiences in infancy and early childhood.

Sigmund Freud recognised the importance of early experience. Like Piaget, he saw development in stages culminating at the time of adolescence. Freud's proposed five stages of which three occurred in early childhood. These were the oral stage (where everything is mouthed); the anal stage (where there is a focus on toilet events) and the phallic stage (which involves interest in the genitals and lasts, Freud suggests, until around the age of six).

The focus of his theory was the role of our unconscious in forming personality and shaping behaviour. He suggested three levels of consciousness:

i.   things we are consciously paying attention to

ii. preconsciousness when we can choose to pay attention, and

iii. subconsciousness – the things in our mind which shape behaviour without us noticing.

Freud saw personality as having three unconscious and conflicting drives or motivational forces:

- the id is especially prevalent in babies when desires have to be met immediately. It is regarded as the instinctive, pleasure-seeking part of our personality;

- the ego develops as the baby comes to realise that what we want cannot or will not always be met. With this realisation the ego develops enabling us to find socially acceptable ways to have our needs met. Freud thought of the ego, as standing between the id (wanting us to be wholly selfish) and the superego (commanding us to be wholly virtuous);

- the superego emerges as we learn about the expectations of parents and society. We might think of it as our conscience.

The conflict that Freud suggests between id, ego and superego causes anxiety and in order to cope with this we develop a variety of defence mechanisms such as repression and denial.

Related key theories

Freud is known as the founding father of psychoanalysis because his ideas influenced the ideas of all who followed him. In this section some key aspects of some other theories are highlighted. Space does not allow a thorough review of these theories, but may help you to become familiar with the leading names and ideas you may come across in your wider reading and discussion. Although some of the ideas developed by those who followed him conflicted with those of Freud himself, all were influenced by his thinking and writing. His ideas permeated and continue to influence thinking about the human mind and emotions.

Carl Jung developed the now everyday idea of extroverts and introverts. He believed that our own unconscious mind, and that of other peoples, shaped developed.

Melanie Klein was mainly interested in children requiring therapy. She believed that play gives children a way of expressing fantasies and reliving experiences symbolically. She worked closely with Susan Isaacs on the Cambridge Evacuation Study during the Second World War. Her work also had a major influence on Winnicott. Klein believed that children used play to symbolise their experiences.

Anna Freud, Sigmund Freud's youngest daughter, worked with her father and, following a period of imprisonment by the Gestapo, was allowed to leave Austria and come to Britain in 1938. Anna Freud's theories were closely based on those of her father but the focus of her work was child psychology. She disagreed with Klein's views on play and its use as a therapy. For her, the major differences between working with children and working with adults were that:

- the relationship with the therapist is different since the parents are still of overwhelming importance to the child;

- children are less able to symbolise or talk about their experiences than adults.

Donald Winnicott was a respected paediatrician and psychoanalyst whose work continues to be influential in Britain and America. His career began in paediatrics but he made many contributions to the development of psychoanalytic theories. Winnicott underlined the importance to children of adult engagement in play[2]. His theories focused heavily on mother and

Narrative can help children to deal with fears

child interactions. He wrote about 'good enough mothers' and highlighted the importance of this relationship. He wrote that the mother's face acted as a mirror for the baby since it revealed what she saw or perceived as she looked at her child. He is also known for recognising the way in which transitional objects, such as a piece of a mother's nightdress, act as a symbol of the mother for a child – helping the child to cope with separation.

Erich Fromm lived in Frankfurt but went to the United States in 1934. His theories were influenced by Sigmund Freud and Karl Marx. He believed that humans have freedom to choose and are not at the mercy of their unconscious motives.

Erik Erikson's ideas are sometimes called psychosocial theory because they cover a life span, with stages running throughout life not ending at adolescence, as do those of Freud and Piaget. Erikson was a pupil and analysand (patient or client) of Anna Freud. He was the first of the psychoanalysts to leave Vienna, following the rise of Nazism. He went to New York, where he had previously studied, and became well respected and widely known. He proposed three systems which make up the development of the individual, namely: the somatic system (related to the body), the ego system (necessary for thinking and reasoning) and the societal system (through which an individual becomes part of their society, culture or community). For Erikson, psychosocial development has eight stages through which all humans pass, each of which has a central dilemma or crisis. Erikson was the first to chart development all the way through to old age, not stopping at adolescence as so many theorists did. The first three stages relate to early childhood and are described more fully in the chart below.

Bruno Bettelheim was an Austrian Jew who was imprisoned by the Nazis. On his release in 1939 he went to America. In 1944 he was

appointed as Professor of Psychology at the University of Chicago. The work for which he is best known is his analysis of fairy tales in terms of Freudian analysis. He highlighted the emotional and symbolic importance of fairy tales for children and suggested that traditional fairy tales allowed children to come to terms with their fears. This, he believed, would enable children to grow and develop emotionally, thus preparing them for a better future.

Putting the theories into practice

Most of the psychoanalytic theorists did not work in practical situations with children. However, the central tenet of many psychoanalytic theories is that children must be supported in working through their emotional or psychological crises in order to develop a sense of emotional wellbeing and mental health. The influence of this fundamental aspect of their work can be seen in many aspects of practice in the early years. The provision made for role play, for example, helps children to play out fears and anxieties. Many group settings acknowledge young children's emotional needs through general free play and providing art materials to encourage creative expression[2].

In day to day work with young children, practitioners are constantly dealing with aspects of the unconscious. Studies have shown[3] that some people attracted to work with young children do so because of their own need for love or attention. In terms of psychoanalysis this may often arise because of needs which have not been fully met in early childhood. This may mean that while things are going well, the work of supporting young children and their families is highly rewarding. However if needs are not met, it may result in feelings of resentment. This may occur, for example, when parents criticise provision or staff fail to agree with or adhere to plans or when children are defiant. In such instances the practitioner may resort to a variety of defence mechanisms. He or she may project negative feelings on to parents or children or colleagues – placing blame on someone else. Alternatively they may regress – becoming childish and difficult or overly dependent on others.

A number of actions, based on the first three stages of Erikson's theory, can support children's healthy development[4]. Practitioners are paying attention to Erikson's stage of:

trust/distrust when they:
- hold babies close and share warm physical contact with them when they are being fed;
- respond quickly when babies are distressed.

autonomy/shame or doubt when they:
- give children simple but genuine choices;
- set clear, consistent and reasonable boundaries;
- accept and understand children's swings between independence and dependence as when toddlers wander off showing independence but keep their parent/carer in view so that they can easily return to the safety that the adult represents.

The first three of Eriksons's eight psychosocial stages of development (for further information see for example http://psychology.about.com/library/bl_psychosocial_summary.htm)

Age	Stage	Central crisis
Birth to one year	trust vs mistrust	The first task is to develop a sense of trust or comfort in their caregivers, environment and self. If this crisis is not resolved they may mistrust themselves and others throughout their lives.
1 to 3 years	autonomy vs shame and doubt	During this stage young children are learning to exercise independence. Shame and doubt about one's own ability to act independently may arise if the child is not supported in making choices and decisions.
3 to 6 years	initiative vs guilt	The young child's developing desire to master the environment. Guilt may arise if the child reacts aggressively or irresponsibly.

initiative/guilt when they:

- encourage children to be independent;
- focus on what children can do, not on the mistakes they make;
- set realistic expectations;
- make the curriculum relevant and based on action.

What does practice look like?

Many, if not most, settings are inevitably influenced by the theories of Freud and his followers. Settings which make a particular effort to engage with such theories will include in their practice:

- recognition of children's need for transitional objects, which enable children to maintain a link with comfortable and familiar people and contexts. Practitioners actively acknowledge the importance of transitional objects, encouraging children to bring their favourite toys and comforters from home as a link between family and setting;

- a key person approach which supports the development of security and intimacy, vital to the healthy development of young children, this is also closely linked to the work of John Bowlby (see page 59);

- reflective practice and staff discussions which help to raise awareness of processes such as projection of feelings and the need for containment and emotional holding. This in turn can enable staff to examine their own feelings and work to deal with parents, each other and children, more positively and effectively;

- supervision for practitioners is built on an understanding of the need for their feelings to be contained. This is particularly true where adults are dealing with issues such as child abuse but also for the daily stress of work with young children and families in need;

- play which is used to enable children to explore and represent feelings and thus come to terms with them. This may take the form of play therapy, developed by Melanie Klein or it may simply be an element of day-to-day practice. Playing hospitals or superheroes allows children to explore both everyday fears and more elemental feelings related to loss and powerlessness;

- opportunities for story telling which enables children to explore feelings. 'Not now Bernard' and 'Bear under the Stairs' are examples of the kinds of books that might be included to support children's emotional development. The support can be extended further by the addition of props such as puppets for children to retell stories in their own words.

The influence of psychoanalytic theories

Freud's theory drew attention to the importance of early experience and the unconscious in relation to the development of personality. His work has inspired many others and led to a new way of viewing human development. This makes it very difficult to quantify the influence of his work but it is possible to say, as the poet Auden said, that Freud changed forever the way we look at everything. Similarly, Freudian slip, is an everyday phrase that alludes to the impact of the subconscious. It is easy to forget that these ideas spring from psychoanalytic theories.

Erikson, Freud's student in Vienna, has been particularly influential, particularly in America. He widened theories of psychosocial development to include the whole life span. He made his theories more educationally relevant by integrating social and cultural factors into his writing. His work also stimulated interest in self-identity and adolescence.

Anna Freud is credited with improving the quality of nursery education and with being instrumental in establishing child guidance services. Melanie Klein was Susan Isaacs' analyst and concern for children's psychological well-being was of vital importance in Susan Isaacs' practice (see page 42). It would be difficult to overestimate the influence that psychoanalytical theorists have had on understanding the role of observation in the care and education of young children.

Winnicott has been highly influential in helping parents and practitioners to recognise the emotional needs of young children particularly at periods of transition. He also developed the notion of a *good enough mother*.

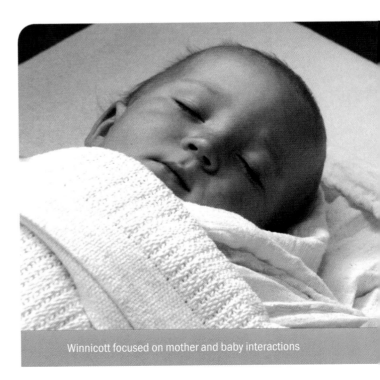

Winnicott focused on mother and baby interactions

Common criticisms of psychoanalytic theories

Freud viewed the development of girls and women from a male perspective, labelling the second stage of development as 'phallic' and thinking of girls' motivation only in terms of 'penis envy'. The developmental aspect of his theories is criticised not merely on feminist grounds but also because of the broader limitations of staged theory (see also Piaget). Freud's work is sometimes criticised for its emphasis on sexual gratification. In fact, for Freud, 'sexual' simply referred to bodily pleasure.

The basis of his and Erikson's theories has been challenged on the grounds that the methods used, such as dream analysis and free association, are not open to scientific verification. Both Freud and Erikson's work could be said to lack coherence. Moreover, the idiosyncratic use of technical terms like generativity or ego makes their work difficult to understand.

It is also clear that the theories of these and other psychotherapists are often misunderstood or misrepresented. While this is not entirely their fault it does mean that the applications of theories can be unhelpful. Susan Isaacs herself was criticised for the free methods which were sometimes seen as chaotic. She struggled with the concept of autonomy when some children were found to be unhappy and discussed the dilemma with Klein. If all children were given the freedom to do as they pleased, the freedoms of other children were constrained.

GLOSSARY

Transitional objects: an object such as a security blanket which comforts a child by providing a link between them and the parent (or other significant people and places).

Projection: a person unconsciously rejects characteristics such as anger or laziness by ascribing them to other people.

Containment: psychologically and emotionally holding the distress of another person in such a way as to allow it to be coped with. This may be described as emotional holding and in early childhood might most easily be thought of in the way in which an adult holds a distressed child. In doing this the child (or patient) can recover without denying or suppressing overwhelming feelings.

Generativity: making your mark on the world, through achieving something worthwhile or helping to make the world a better place in some way. Erikson attributed this to adulthood and contrasted it with stagnation.

Defence mechanisms: strategies used to avoid dealing with uncomfortable memories or experiences.

POINTS FOR REFLECTION

- Think of a situation where you have used a defence mechanism. What impact did this have on you and others?

- Identify some books or stories that you use to help children deal with emotional issues.

- What help needs to be available for parents to understand and support their children's emotional well-being?

Expression of anger is seen as a safety valve

John Dewey

PROFILE

John Dewey's approach sounds strangely modern, as he sought, through his work in his laboratory school, to find answers to questions we are still struggling with today.

KEY DATES

1859	Born in Burlington, Vermont, USA
1884	Awarded PhD at John Hopkins University
1896	Establishes laboratory school at the University of Chicago
1904	Moves to Columbia University, New York City
1952	Dies

LINKS

Froebel
McMillan
Isaacs
Montessori
Vygotsky

Knowledge develops in the environment

- *Democracy and Education* (Free Press, 1916)

- *How We Think: a Reinstatement of the Relation of Reflective Thinking to the Educative Process* (Henry Regnery, 1933)

His life

John Dewey was born in 1859 in Vermont into a family of farmers. After gaining a PhD at John Hopkins University he became a professor of philosophy at the University of Michigan. In 1886 he married one of his students, Alice Chipman, and they worked together to explore ways of improving education. Eight years later they moved to Chicago where Dewey took a job teaching philosophy, psychology and educational theory. He established a laboratory school there which attracted worldwide attention.

His writing

John Dewey's best known publications include:

- *My Pedagogic Creed* (1897) which set out many of his ideas[1]

- *School for Tomorrow*, with Evelyn Dewey (Dutton, 1915)

His theory

Dewey's philosophy or theory is known as pragmatism. He favoured a naturalistic approach that saw knowledge as developing as humans adapt to their environment. He rejected the term *epistemology*, which was favoured by Piaget and preferred to think of learning as a theory of inquiry or *experimental logic*.

Dewey's theory was that:

- children learn by doing and by being active (a view developed by Froebel);

- education should be based on real-life situations including interaction with others (as advocated by Vygotsky);

- experimentation and independent thinking should be fostered. He saw children as being characterised by curiosity, similarly to scientists.

Aspects of Dewey's theory and practice linked to his writing

Key aspect of Dewey's theory and practice	Dewey's words from *My Pedagogic Creed*
Importance of social interaction.	True education comes through the stimulation of the child's powers by the demands of the social situations in which he finds himself.
Need to develop the curriculum from children's interests.	The child's own instinct and powers furnish the material and give the starting point for all education.
As long as people are alive they are learning.	I believe that education... is a process of living and not preparation for future living.
The value and culture of family and community should be reflected in the life of the school.	The school life should grow gradually out of the home life.... it is the business of the school to deepen and extend the child's sense of values bound up in his home.
Teachers are not just teaching children as individuals they are helping children to live in society and shaping society as a whole.	I believe that the teacher is engaged, not simply in the training of individuals, but in the formation of a proper social life.
Children work on ideas and finding solutions in what is termed 'project method'.	Many so-called projects are of such a short time-span and are entered upon for such casual reasons, that extension of acquaintance with facts and principles is at a minimum. In short, they are too trivial to be educative.

Projects can promote curiosity

Putting the theory into practice

Questions that Dewey struggled to answer in his observations, lectures and writings included[1]:

- How do we best introduce children to subject matter?
- Should we have mixed age classes?
- How can we best plan?
- How can support staff and teachers work best together?
- How should children be taught to think?

At the heart of Dewey's view of education are teachers who:

- have good general knowledge;
- know their children well;
- want to continue learning;
- observe children and plan from what they learn of them;
- are able to develop reflective practice.

What does practice look like?

Dewey is most closely associated with a project approach, developing cross-curricular ways of learning. Mooney[1] gives an example of what she claims Dewey would regard as 'an educational experience'. She describes a kindergarten where the teacher had invited a parent to come and make ice cream with the children. The recipe had been in the family for generations. The mother took the children to a nearby lake and the old ice house which had been used before the days of refrigeration and helped them to make ice cream as it had been made 'in the olden days'. Children discussed their favourite ice creams and visited a factory – they took photographs, drew pictures, collected recipes and followed up a host of interests.

The teacher's role is described as follows[1]:

'The teacher observed and asked questions to find out what the children already knew. She set up experiences for them to discover things they didn't already know. She used her knowledge of development to plan curriculum that was age appropriate and she documented the children's learning to support her understanding of their thinking. The success of the project is measured by the fact that it led into the next area of study. The children were left curious, wanting more, and confident in their ability to dive in and satisfy their curiosity.'

Experimentation should be fostered

For Dewey having fun is not enough. He wanted children to have opportunities to:

- develop their own interests. While this is often regarded as a way of motivating children for Dewey it was essential to enable children to discover the relationship between knowledge and experience;

- work in ways that match their age and stage of development;

- engage in activities and experiences which contribute to their understanding and appreciation of their world.

His influence

The many progressive educational movements which sprang up in England in the first half of the twentieth century acknowledged their debt to Dewey. Susan Isaacs, for example, admired his work. His work influenced a government report (the *Hadow Report on Nursery and Infant Schools*) published in 1933 and more than 30 years later, in 1967, there were echoes of his influence in

The Plowden Report. In 1897, Dewey had written 'I believe that education... is a process of living and not preparation for future living'. Seventy years later, *The Plowden Report* stated, in remarkably similar language, that 'a school is not merely a teaching shop... it is a community in which children learn to live first and foremost as children and not as future adults'.

Dewey is said to have been responsible for project approaches linking learning across the curriculum. Current emphasis on planning from children's interests are very much in line with Dewey's theory. He has also been credited with developing the notion of reflective professional practice[2].

He made a distinction between 'routinised' and 'reflective' teaching and he identified stages in reflection which include:

- perplexity, confusion, doubt;

- a tentative interpretation;

- a careful survey;

- a consequent elaboration; and

- testing the hypothesis.

Common criticisms of his theory

As Dewey himself recognised, project approaches have been criticised as leading to trivialisation. This might occur if the other aspects of Dewey's philosophy, such as observation and reflective practice, are not given enough weight. The reflective practitioner would guard against trivialisation by evaluating learning. There have also been political criticisms since Dewey's emphasis on the democratisation of education have sometimes been seen as unhelpful or unnecessary – although his work is highly influential in China.

Some criticisms have been made of his use of language and technical terms. This criticism is by no means limited to Dewey's work – it is a common fault amongst academic writers.

GLOSSARY

Pragmatism: a philosophy that truth is not about relationship to facts but about the extent to which an idea matches experience.

POINTS FOR REFLECTION

○ Consider Dewey's stages of reflection. How do they compare or apply to your reflective practice?

○ Dewey did not regard himself as offering child-centred education because he believed that gave adults an insufficient role. He felt that adults should be "the intellectual leader of a social group". Do you agree? If so how do you achieve this?

○ Dewey believed that education is the key to social progress. What aspects of practice in your setting reflect this?

Care needs to be taken to ensure that project work does not trivialise thinking and investigation

Margaret McMillan

PROFILE

Some argue that Margaret McMillan invented the nursery school. At the beginning of the twentieth century, with her sister Rachel, she set up an open-air camp to nurture underprivileged children. From this she developed the idea of the nursery school with open access to a garden.

KEY DATES

1860	Born in New York, USA
1865	Moves to Scotland with her mother and sister
1883	Goes to England to work as governess
1894	Elected to the Bradford School Board
1903	Becomes manager of the Deptford Centre
1917	Sister Rachel dies
1923	Elected President of the Nursery Schools Association
1930	Rachel McMillan Training College opens
1931	Dies in Harrow

LINKS

Froebel
Owen
Steiner

Health was seen as key to learning and development

Her life

Margaret McMillan and her older sister, Rachel, were born in New York after her parents had emigrated there from Scotland. In 1865, both her younger sister, aged three, and her father died of scarlet fever in 1865. Margaret survived the illness but it left her deaf. She did not recover her hearing until she was 14. Their mother took Rachel and Margaret back to Scotland, where they lived with her parents in Inverness. McMillan later wrote that it was as though their mother was ashamed of widowhood and that she 'passed into shadow'.

Motivated by her strong Christian and Socialist beliefs and deeply moved by the plight of families suffering during the London dock strike of 1889, Margaret started to take an interest in politics, writing a series of articles for the *Christian Socialist* magazine. She wrote about things that preoccupied her for the rest of her life – the plight of the poor and their ability to change their lives. She also joined the Fabian Society, a left-wing political group, and was soon speaking all over the country. She soon gained a reputation both as an orator and advocate for the poor. In 1893, McMillan found a job teaching adult education in Bradford and became a member of the Independent Labour Party. In 1894, she was elected onto the Bradford School Board. Her arrival in Bradford coincided with a period of high unemployment. McMillan was appalled on her visits to schools by the poverty that children lived in. She described the children as dirty, ill-fed and wretched. She began to advise parents on hygiene and nutrition and became a local expert in the health, education and well-being of young children. McMillan took on more lecture tours – she was a charismatic speaker – and continued with her political writing.

Her writing

Margaret McMillan began writing towards the end of the nineteenth century. Her writings – books and articles – focused on young children and had a Christian and a socialist slant. In 1904 she wrote *Education through the Imagination* – a book greatly admired by Rudolf Steiner, and followed this with *The Economic Aspects of Child Labour and Education* in 1905. Her most influential book in this country has perhaps been *The Nursery School* (first published in 1919 and revised in 1930).

Her theory

The theories which led Margaret McMillan and her sister, Rachel, to work with young children were rooted in action. Their political and religious beliefs led them to look for ways of alleviating the effects of poverty. In the 1900s, McMillan's work focused on the national medical inspection of children. In 1901, she resigned from the Bradford School Board, following a period of illness, and moved to London, where her sister Rachel was working in a home for young girls. Their interest in the physical health of working class families was widely shared. A high proportion of the recruits to fight in the Boer War were deemed unfit and this alerted many to the poor health of poor families, and alarmed them.

In addition to focusing on what the sisters regarded as remedial action, they had a strong philosophical base to their beliefs and theories in which three strands were paramount:

- the promotion of fairness and social justice at the heart of all they did (influenced by socialism);

- a drive to change things for the better (influenced by their religious faith);

- a desire to harness the power of nature and the beauty of simplicity (influenced by Froebel and by creative thinkers of the day such as John Ruskin and William Morris).

It has been suggested[1] that McMillan's education theories were based on those of Robert Owen. In 1902 she became a member of the Froebel Society's council and was undoubtedly influenced by Froebel's work. It is also argued that the theories of progressive educators such as John Dewey also influenced her thinking. Interestingly, McMillan disagreed with aspects of Montessori's theory as she believed it placed insufficient emphasis on imagination – a view she shared with Steiner.

Putting the theory into practice

The work of the sisters focused first on health, for they believed that without tackling these issues children would be unable to learn and develop. In 1903, McMillan became manager of a group of Deptford schools and wrote articles to educate the public about child development, physiology and hygiene. She opened a small experimental clinic at Bow, funded by a wealthy American philanthropist. This later moved to Deptford where it served a group of schools. The Deptford

The McMillan sisters developed the School Meals Service

Centre included a clinic. Small operations, such as the removal of adenoids, could be carried out there and a remedial gym improved children's health and strength. From 1911 the provision included a night camp which aimed to improve the health of children in danger of contracting tuberculosis. For nine months of the year, girls between the ages of six and 14 were able to sleep outdoors in a churchyard. By 1914, the number of places available had trebled and boys were included.

An open-air baby camp, catering for 29 young children, had been set up. By 1917, the Rachel McMillan Nursery School had been established, with places for 100 children. There was a strong emphasis on being outdoors. The classrooms were, and still are, (the school is part of the Royal Borough of Greenwich's early years provision) called shelters; there was a large and attractive garden and even when the weather was bad, the classroom verandahs gave children the chance to benefit from fresh air and space. A medical supervisor reported on the marked improvement in children's physical and mental well-being. By the end of the First World War, Margaret McMillan was considered an expert in nursery education and in 1923 she was elected president of the Nursery Schools Association.

What does practice look like?

In her book, The Nursery School, McMillan wrote that hundreds of thousands of children were in dire need of education and nurture in the early years. She provided a mixture of care and education – the school was open from 8.00am until 5.30pm. She believed children performed badly at school because they were poorly prepared for learning in the early years. She stressed that in the open-air nursery children had no examinations to sit, no formal structure to the day but had time to play, to run free in open spaces, feel the sun and the wind and explore the natural world. In 1930, the year before she died, Margaret McMillan set up a training college, adjacent to the Rachel McMillan Nursery School. Teacher training continued at the college for around 50 years.

The nursery school in Deptford that Margaret McMillan developed and named after her sister Rachel, has large and beautiful gardens. The 'shelters' or classrooms were built with verandahs and with windows that folded back so that the rooms were light and airy. They all had a bath. McMillan wrote that 'Children want space at all ages. But from the age of one to seven, space, that is ample space, is almost as much wanted as food and air. To move, to run, to find things out by new movement, to feel one's life in every limb, that is the life of early childhood'.[2]

The free play associated with Froebel was encouraged here but McMillan felt that neither Froebel nor Pestalozzi had faced up to the problems that affected the lives of the poor. She wrote that[2] children needed experience 'just as they need food... gay and varied music and dancing, with tales and play but above all free movement and experience'. A routine of regular meals and sleep times was established as well as times for children to run and play.

Her influence

Margaret and Rachel McMillan had many political allies and were highly influential. Their high profile brought the needs of young children to the attention of many who might not otherwise have been interested in or concerned about nurseries. The establishment of the school medical service and the school meals service, which were brought about through the work of the McMillans, had a long-lasting impact in the UK. Their emphasis on the nursery school as an open-air institution influenced how nursery schools were built throughout the first half of the twentieth century. The overall approach adopted by Margaret McMillan was seen as exemplary. The work of the school in Deptford was praised in a government report on nursery education published in 1933 (the Hadow Report on Nursery and Infant Schools).

Common criticisms of her theory

The McMillan sisters believed that greater economies could be achieved through large-scale institutions and that there was likely to be more widespread provision if it was not too expensive. Others thought it was inappropriate for young children to be in large institutions. The school in Deptford, for example, at one stage catered for 500 children.

Criticisms were also made of the long hours offered at the school, which was open from 8.00 in the morning until 5.30 each day. This, with the apparently middle class values displayed in the school, such as putting flowers on the table, was seen by some as professionalising parenting.

When McMillan was elected president of the Nursery Schools Association in 1923, she suggested that all children from two to seven years of age who are in day care settings should be looked after by fully qualified specialist teachers. She wrote that: 'Underlying all mental and bodily development lies the need for free activity. Without it neither healthy growth of body and spirit, nor training in self-control is possible... Free activity involves the provision of spontaneous and purposeful activity in spacious open air conditions ... as well as an atmosphere of love, joy and freedom... the daily routine must provide for the right alternation of rest and activity through the day... it is undesirable to accept the hours of the ordinary school day as the limit for nursery school'.

POINTS FOR REFLECTION

○ 'Time and space' was the unofficial motto for the nursery school. Why do you think the McMillan sisters regarded this as so important?

○ What are children learning when they use their imagination?

○ What is the importance of physical movement in young children's learning and development?

Rudolf Steiner and Steiner Waldorf education

PROFILE

Rudolf Steiner, an Austrian scientist and philosopher, established new forms of architecture, medicine and education. Steiner Waldorf schools provide a distinctive form of education that fosters personal and social development and is based on the view of the child as a spiritual being.

KEY DATES

1861	Born in Austria
1919	First Steiner Waldorf school established
1925	Dies
1925	First Steiner Waldorf school opens in England

LINKS

McMillan

His life

Rudolf Steiner was born in the village of Kraljevec, Austria (now Croatia). At university he concentrated on maths, physics and chemistry but wrote his final thesis on philosophy. He worked first in Weimar and then Berlin, where he was involved in publishing. He gave courses on history and natural science and offered practical training in public speaking.

Steiner was interested in spirituality and established a 'science of the spirit', that he called anthroposophy. Albert Schweitzer, an early twentieth century philosopher, was impressed by Steiner's philosophical writings and views. A World Anthroposophical Society still exists with its headquarters in Switzerland and followers throughout the world, especially in the United States of America. Anthroposophy is concerned with the human struggle for inner freedom.

Impressed by the breadth and depth of his thinking, the director of the Waldorf-Astoria cigarette factory in Stuttgart, Emil Molt, asked Steiner to form a school for both the children of workers and for the children of more wealthy families. Two years later, in 1919 the first Steiner Waldorf school was founded. From this modest beginning, there are today 1,800 kindergartens and 900 schools situated in all five continents of the world.

His writing

Rudolf Steiner wrote around 30 books and gave an estimated 6,000 lectures across Europe. The Steiner Waldorf Fellowship, Rudolf Steiner Press and the Anthroposophic Press have published some of Steiner's writings and collections of his lectures. The topics he covered in his writing include spiritual and philosophical matters, art, music, literature, art, science and nature and economics. Of this vast range of writing, those most relevant to early childhood care and education are perhaps:

- *The Education of the Child in the Light of Anthroposophy*, republished in 1995 by the Rudolf Steiner Publishing Company

- *The Education of the Child*, published by Anthroposophic Press (originally published in 1907)

- *The Kingdom of Childhood* published by Rudolf Steiner Press (originally published in 1924)

- *The child's changing consciousness and Waldorf education* published by Rudolf Steiner Press in 1988 (drawn from lectures given during 1923)

His theory

Rudolf Steiner wanted to create an education which gave children clarity of thought, sensitivity of feeling and strength of will. Steiner's theory centred on all aspects of growth and development including spirituality. He aimed for all children to experience both arts and sciences and a balanced experience of what he described as 'thinking, feeling and willing'. Steiner's philosophy sprang from the idea that there are three seven-year cycles of development. Education needs to work with the unfolding abilities and changing needs of the child at each stage. These stages are described as follows:

- from birth to seven the active, or will, predominates;

Interaction with nature underlines the rhythm of the seasons

- from seven to 14 the affective, or feeling, predominates;

- from 14 to 21 the cognitive, or thinking ability, predominates.

Steiner believed that children who have suffered from pressure to succeed intellectually at too early an age often lack the motivation to learn for themselves. The avoidance of formal learning springs from a desire to protect the faculties of feeling and willing.

Steiner Waldorf education includes a number of key elements which underpin practice. These theoretical ideas include:

- The importance of imitation and imagination. For Steiner, imitation was the prime means of learning. It is closely linked to the development of the will (see glossary) since no one can insist that children imitate others – they can only choose or will that for themselves. In watching adults, children become willing to try out similar actions. Imagination is important in Steiner Waldorf education because it is linked to the underpinning philosophy or anthroposophy (see glossary). It involves conjuring up things which are not present to the senses.

- A focus on what have been described[1] as the 3Rs of Steiner education – rhythm; repetition and reverence. It is believed that rhythm helps children to contain their energy and guides their movements at a stage in their lives when they find this difficult. Rhythm underpins every aspect of Steiner Waldorf practice since it is seen as key to helping children feel confident, strong and secure. Repetition is also used to increase children's sense of stability and security as well as to support learning and memory. Reverence or respect is for other people, the environment and for food. It is also for each child as an individual. Practitioners describe this in a variety of terms such as 'reverence for the child', 'respect for the child's journey' or 'reading the book of the child'. This reverence goes far beyond observation and involves seeking to gain through intuition and reflection a full picture of each child.

Putting the theory into practice

The environment in Steiner Waldorf schools is carefully structured to foster personal and social development. During the early years, teaching is by example and learning is cross-curricular without subject boundaries. The pace of learning is set by the child. Imagination and imitation are nurtured through play. Play strengthens the imagination and supports all aspects of development. It also enables children to concentrate, be inventive and adaptable. Steiner teachers believe that these faculties are at their peak from birth to seven and are the main way of learning. They are therefore fostered and respected. Adults do not engage directly in children's play but create an environment which supports imitation and imagination – with open ended play materials such as cones and pebbles. Equipment is intended to be used flexibly – children in one kindergarten for example built a hotel by placing three tables on top of one another – each table being a room in the hotel.

The general structure of the day highlights the importance of repetition and rhythm. The pattern of the day is predictable. The rhythm of the seasons is highlighted through festivals and through gardening experiences. The reverence for food is demonstrated through shared mealtimes and children's active engagement in food preparation. Steiner Waldorf practitioners argue that children need the reassurance of continuity and that regular events should punctuate the year, week and day. Seasonal activities celebrate the cycles of the year. Each week has its own regular rhythm of recurring activities – baking day, painting day, gardening day. Every day has its own smaller rhythms. These are believed to help the child feel secure and know what to expect; a tidy-up song for example might signal the end of one activity and the start of another. Each day has a special time – a quiet moment to experience reverence. There is a rhythmic shift between the child's time (creative play, outside time) and the teacher's time (circle time, story), which in the early years is kept short. Steiner believed that working with rhythm helps children to live with change, to find their place in the world and to begin to understand the past, present and future. The repetition establishes continuity and aids the development of memory which is strengthened by recurring experiences. Daily, weekly and yearly events are remembered and anticipated a second time around. Stories are told not just once but many times.

Repetition supports learning and memory

Overall, there is an emphasis on practical experiences such as gardening, cooking, cleaning and an expectation that children will learn from adults as they bake bread, sew and generally go about their daily work. Up to the age of seven, teachers avoid showing children printed words. Formal schooling does not begin until this age but learning is supported in everything that is going on. Mathematics, for example, might be demonstrated through cooking. Thinly sliced carrots make natural circles. Carrots can be cut, chopped, cubed and counted before being eaten in soup. All mathematical activities arise naturally in response to the demands of the day: flour is weighed, plates and bowls are counted, food is shared. Mathematics is encountered, not in abstract but in practical, human terms.

There is a focus on the spoken word. Stories are told rather than read, many times over – creating an appreciation of the human voice and the beauty and rhythm of language, extending vocabulary and supporting the development of memory and imagination. Steiner teachers believe that stories, songs, poems, puppets and movement provide the best possible introduction to literacy. During each day some time is dedicated to free creative play. Songs, stories, poems and puppet shows together with eurhythmy – a system of movement with language and music that is characteristic of Steiner approaches – are all seen as contributing to children's development.

What does practice look like?

The Steiner Waldorf kindergarten is designed to be a warm and friendly place with a homelike environment. Parental involvement is high. The physical environment is important. 'The teacher attempts to engage the child's whole being in what they do, in as an artistic way as possible, by providing a warm and joyful environment in which the child can feel nurtured and at ease, happy to explore and play, be busy and be still... The room is painted and in a warm colour, has few hard rectangular corners, and is often furnished with soft muslins to mark off a different area, or draped over a window to give a softer quality of light. The quality of sound is that of human voices rather than of mechanical toys. The materials in the room are natural and are at children's level, and stored in aesthetic containers such as simple baskets or wooden boxes which may themselves be incorporated into the play[2].'

Although adults do not actively engage in children's play they are thoroughly 'present'. As they sit with children they knit or sew or prepare vegetables – watching and encouraging, available if needed and ready to listen. Some children may be involved in the same activity as the adult. The day is carefully structured and although children have a great deal of freedom in their play, the tidying up session is well-managed with clear rules. For example, in story-telling adults use pieces of coloured muslin – blue may denote sky or sea, green may denote grass. Children are encouraged to imitate the use of fabric and develop their own imaginative ideas using the fabric. At the end of the session, one tidy-up task is to fold and roll the pieces of material that have been used – a routine which is both rhythmic and repetitive and which structures children's actions.

His influence

The philosophy which underpins the work of Steiner Waldorf schools is widely respected. Its emphasis on imaginative play and not introducing children to print until they are seven is seen as flying in the face of mainstream practice which favours an early introduction to books. It provides food for thought for reflective practitioners, encouraging them to pause and reconsider why they do what they do[4]. Some current research[5] suggests that there are no benefits to an early start in reading.

In a similar vein it might be useful to consider the emphasis placed on imitation by Steiner Waldorf practitioners. Recent research on so-called mirror neurons has highlighted the importance of imitation in learning from birth and throughout life. This is, of course, not something that Steiner could have known since no such research existed.

Above all, perhaps, Steiner's ideas have kept alive a respect for children and childhood. The quotes below give a flavour of the impact of that sense of reverence:

> Steiner philosophy has kept alive the belief that children do not have to begin to read at 5, do not have to use a computer before they can walk. It has challenged the over-protection of children by enabling 2-year-olds to cut with real knives and 6-year-olds to whittle with sharp implements... they have kept the faith in and with children.[6]

> It seems to me that Steiner educators express in every line and every utterance their fundamental trust, in both children and adults. They trust in the pedagogical value of what children spontaneously do in their play, in a harmonious and supporting environment; ... and they trust as completely in the value of their own, adults activities – their story telling, their sewing, their music-making, their calm, sensitive watchfulness, their joyful loving presences – as they consciously shape the environment in which the children learn by living.[7]

Common criticisms of his theory

- Late introduction to literacy. Children have enormous understanding of print at a very early stage – they see words in their environment not just in books. To ignore this in the early years could be seen as not recognising and building on children's previous experience. However, there is evidence (see previous section) that a late start may have benefits.

- Unwillingness to engage with the early years prescribed curriculum. The absence of clear academic aims is at odds with current mainstream practice. It may be seen as indulgent and insufficiently challenging and yet accounts of practice identify high levels of engagement in play and imaginative activity as well as everyday activities, such as cooking. A Guide to the Early Years Foundation Stage in Steiner Waldorf Early Childhood Settings

has been produced[3] alerting practitioners to areas in which their practice is in line with that prescribed by government.

- Resistance to the use of technology in the early years. Steiner Waldorf education rejects the use of the technology which most children encounter at home and in their early childhood setting. Practitioners do however make use of what they term 'warm' technology – hand driven devices such as spinning wheels and apple presses, where children can see how the machine works. Steiner Waldorf practitioners are not alone in questioning the widespread use of technology with young children. For example, Robin Alexander, who led a review of the primary curriculum; the acclaimed neuroscientist Susan Greenfield; and many speech therapists also challenge unthinking use of technology.

GLOSSARY

Anthroposophy: a form of philosophy which seeks to develop modes of thinking which involve imagination, inspiration and intuition.

Eurythmy: a form of movement, used throughout Steiner Waldorf school, beginning in the kindergarten. It is used to enable children to visualise and internalise sounds, linking thought and movement. (For a fuller explanation see Nicol, 2007, which is listed in the suggestions for further reading.)

Willing: a term used by Steiner practitioners to emphasise the importance of doing but with reference to choices that children make of their own free will.

POINTS FOR REFLECTION

- What steps could you take to make your setting calmer? What would be your reasons for wanting to do this?

- List the pros and cons of the later start to formal schooling which Steiner Waldorf education favours.

- Try to find out why some speech therapists question the use of television, computer games and videos with very young children.

Maria Montessori and the Montessori method

PROFILE

Maria Montessori was the first woman in Italy to receive a medical degree. She is famous for developing an approach to early childhood education that still carries her name.

KEY DATES

1870	Born in Ancona, Italy
1896	Graduates as the first female doctor in Italy
1907	Opens first Casa Dei Bambini (children's house) in Rome
1913	100 Montessori schools in USA
1922	Becomes government inspector of schools in Rome
1934	Leaves Italy to escape from Mussolini's Fascist regime
1952	Dies in the Netherlands

LINKS

Froebel
Isaacs
McMillan

Her life

Montessori's father was a soldier and later a civil servant. Her mother was from a wealthy family and well educated. Montessori was a diligent student, good at mathematics. She enrolled at the University of Rome to become a doctor – unheard of for a woman in Italy at that time. On graduating, she became an assistant at San Giovanni Hospital. She developed an interest in the welfare of deprived children and in particular what were then called 'idiot children'. Study of the writings of Edouard Seguin about mentally defective children sparked her interest in education.

By the age of thirty, Maria Montessori was already well known and respected as a physician and as an educator. She had received a prestigious award for outstanding services to hospitals and was the director of a school in Rome, teaching and training in the care and education of mentally deficient children. In that same year, 1900, she gave birth to an illegitimate son, which led to her withdrawal from many aspects of public life. The father of her child was a colleague, but she did not fully acknowledge her son until her death in 1952.

Although she began to study anthropology, experimental psychology, educational psychology and educational philosophy, she began to visit elementary schools to see how children were being taught. She came to believe that the methods of education which she developed in her work with children with mental disability were appropriate for all children.

In 1907 Montessori established her first Casa dei Bambini, or children's house, in Rome. Her book, *The Montessori Method*, describes every aspect of a child's life at Montessori school, from what the child should eat for lunch to how the teachers should dress and how the room should be set out. The book was widely read and translations were published in various countries. In 1911, Montessori visited America. Educators travelled from all over the world to visit the Casa dei Bambini. The first English Montessori class was established by Bertram Hawker in Norfolk.

At the age of 40, Maria gave up all other work to devote her life to what had become a business, Montessori movement – copyrighting and certifying materials, giving lectures and writing. Her first visit to London was in 1919. Greeted like a celebrity, newspapers described her arrival as the beginning of a great era for children in this country. Two thousand people applied for 250 places available on her first training course. Montessori was particularly popular in Holland where her approach was used in both public and private schools there.

Amsterdam became the headquarters of the Montessori movement and it was in Holland that she died of a brain haemorrhage, just a few months before her 82nd birthday.

Her writing

Montessori published a wide range of medical papers. Her educational method is described in detail in her book *The Montessori Method* (published in 1912 by Heinemann). Other publications include *The Absorbent Mind*, ABC Clio Ltd, 1988. (First published in 1949.)

Independence and self-direction are fostered

Her theory

Montessori read all the major works on educational theory of the previous 200 years and was influenced by Rousseau, Pestalozzi and Froebel. She disagreed with Rousseau's notion of unstructured learning and running wild but agreed with him on the importance of the senses in learning and development. As a doctor, Montessori had seen at first hand the inhumane treatment of children with learning disabilities, often simply placed amongst adults deemed insane and this convinced her of the need for special schools for mentally disabled and emotionally disturbed children.

Montessori was perhaps the first theorist to claim that her philosophy and approach were based on scientific methods. Using her observations of children, she drew the conclusion that education begins from birth and that children are naturally eager to learn. She aimed to harness children's natural ability to learn and emphasised the importance of concrete experiences and materials to help children to understand abstract principles.

Her observations suggested to her that children:

- learn through movement, particularly the movement of the hand which she believed was linked to the development of intelligence;

- enjoy learning in an environment designed to meet their needs;

- learn best through the senses, which she believed lay the foundations for intellectual understanding;

- reveal a spontaneous self-discipline within a prepared environment;

- respond best to educational opportunities in an environment which is prepared to meet their special sensitivities for learning. She claimed that children have 'sensitive periods' when their senses are optimally ready to learn new ideas which she believed included movement coordination; the development of language; and social development.

She also suggested that there were four main developmental stages or, as she termed them, planes. These were early childhood, from conception to six years of age; childhood from 6 to 12; adolescence from 12 to 18 and early adulthood from 18 to 24. In early childhood, "the child's absorbent mind assimilates information effortlessly, creatively exploring through their senses. It is a phase of self-creation when the child begins to develop their own view of the world within their culture"[3].

Putting the theory into practice

Setting up the first Casa dei Bambini or children's house in a slum district of Rome was part of an urban regeneration project. The children there were given simple things to play with and the staff were told only to observe children in self-directed activity and not to intervene. Montessori was astonished at the results – children who had been sullen and withdrawn started to show interest in the objects they had been given to play with. There were wooden cylinders which fitted into a stand, cubes to build into a tower and different shapes to fit into holes on a wooden tray. Staff noticed that children became absorbed in these objects and preferred to play with them rather than the dolls and balls or little wagons. Montessori described the children as changing from timid and wild to social, communicative and joyous. What is now known as the Montessori method, began as responses to the observations made of children in the Casa dei Bambini. Over time Montessori opened more Casa dei Bambini and extended her methods to older children and to children from more affluent families.

A number of key themes underpin Montessori education. These include:

● *Adults' observation and respect for the child as a unique individual*. Montessori wrote that 'the child can only be free when the adult becomes an acute observer. Any action of the adult that is not a response to the children's observed behaviour limits the child's freedom'[1].

Daily living skills are a vital part of the curriculum

● *Independence*. The Montessori classroom accommodates children of mixed ages and is designed to meet children's needs at periods when they are most interested and motivated. This, together with the ordered environment supports independence.

● *Active learning and self-direction*. Children are encouraged to spend relatively long uninterrupted periods of time in which to follow their interests or to carry out their tasks. Montessori wrote that "children need a cycle of work for which they have been mentally prepared; such intelligent work with interest is not fatiguing and they should not be arbitrarily cut off from it by a call to play. Interest is not immediately born, and if when it has been created, the work is withdrawn, it is like depriving a whetted appetite of the food that will satisfy it"[2].

Her influence

Montessori's influence continues to be immense, her approach described as the world's largest educational movement. Those who work in Montessori schools claim that the method produces children who are decision-makers, confident and independent. The Montessori method continues to be favoured around the world, offering structure and clear guidance to practitioners. There are around 22,000 Montessori schools around the world. In Britain there are over 600, catering for over 30,000 children.

In her lifetime, Montessori was feted. When she came to London in 1919, a large reception was held at the Savoy. She was invited to lecture widely and the courses she offered were oversubscribed. Her influence continued in London schools up to the Second World War. Montessori equipment and the small-scale furniture she introduced were to be found in infant schools throughout the city. Susan Isaacs initially resourced her school with Montessori equipment – but later abandoned it in favour of less structured approaches.

Leaving Italy when Mussolini was in power, Montessori expressed the view that if the education of young children included more democratic processes such as choice and independence, people would be less likely to follow a fascist dictator. This is a view that Dewey would have shared.

Common criticisms of her theory

The prescriptive nature of the Montessori method is often criticised. It cannot be easily adapted or updated. One of the greatest difficulties with the method is its apparent rejection of the role of play and imagination in learning. This may be explained by the fact that Montessori was dealing with severely disadvantaged children. She believed that they needed to learn through meaningful tasks and that imaginative play would distract them from the real world. Modern day practitioners suggest that from the Montessori perspective, 'play is work' and 'work is play': both involve freedom of choice, decision-making and deep engagement, which promote concentration[3].

What does practice look like?

Maria Montessori introduced small-scale furniture for children. She had child-sized lightweight furniture, including little armchairs and washstands, specially made. Gardening, gymnastics, caring for plants and pets were added to the daily activities. The children were free to move about and to choose what interested them, within certain boundaries set down by the staff. Materials were placed so that children could get out and use the equipment they needed.

The curriculum in today's Montessori nurseries is based on Montessori's principles of education. It aims to support all aspects of the child's personal and social development. The main curriculum areas are:

- *Daily living skills*, which aim to provide foundations for learning centred around care for the environment; care for oneself as an individual; and care for others in the community. The purpose is to promote independence, and children undertake tasks such as cleaning, tidying and dressing. The tasks also support the development of fine and gross motor skills.

- *Education of the senses*. The aim is to develop skills for learning through taste, smell, hearing sight and touch. By observing, understanding and exploring the world, the child learns how to classify, discriminate, evaluate and sequence. Children sort objects into size order and explore links between two and three dimensional forms.

- *Communication, language and literacy*. Montessori believed that children can learn to read, write (and count) at an early age.

However, she also believed that these should only be introduced when children showed interest, and that teachers should be ready to spot these times in a child's development. Montessori education addresses all four aspects of language– spoken language, listening, writing and reading. Self-expression and communication are regarded as vital elements of all four. A characteristic of Montessori teaching is the phonetic method which is used to teach the sounds of the letters of the alphabet followed by word building exercises which lead to phonetic reading, then total reading. Montessori developed methods of teaching children letters (and numbers) by cutting out shapes in sandpaper.

- *Mathematics*. The focus is on providing a concrete understanding of the concepts of number and mathematics in the environment. The structure of the decimal system is emphasised as children's understanding increases.

- *Cultural aspects of life and understanding of the world*. This includes botany, zoology, history and geography. It also includes science and exploration of the wider world which aims to provide experiences of the natural world including the plant and animal kingdoms, people, events and cultures.

- *Self-expression*. Children are given the opportunity to experience and create in areas relating to cultures – art, music, craft, drama, dance and physical education. These aspects are said to enable children to develop their imaginative responses and their creative self-expression. Activities may include painting, the use of natural materials and access to tuned and untuned percussion instruments.

Susan Isaacs was critical of the approach to reading that Montessori advocated, quoting Stern as saying that 'it is the paucity of other games in the Montessori schools which makes the children take to this new occupation. In the Froebel kindergartens, with their incomparably greater variety of occupations to exercise the child's powers of intuition and imagination, his interest and independence, as a general rule, scarcely any instances of liking for reading and writing exercise are to be observed'[4]. Currently, the early introduction of more formal methods in many schools has given a more established place to phonics in the early years and is welcomed by some, though not all, practitioners and policy makers.

Montessori's focus on sensitive periods, although supported by other theorists such as Steiner, is not wholly supported by neuroscience. It does seem clear that motor development, language and emotional attachment do have a relatively narrow period of time during which they ought to be developed. However, few children are exposed to the extremes which prevent normal development in these areas. Brain studies indicate that human brains are remarkably resilient and can usually recover from the deprivations that threaten development. Attachment in infancy may be an exception to this – perhaps the only learning that cannot readily be compensated for later in life.

GLOSSARY

Planes: developmental stages.

Sensitive periods: critical ages or stages within which children develop most effectively within particular areas or aspects.

POINTS FOR REFLECTION

- Montessori's practices can be found in many aspects of early childhood education today. List some of the things you noticed in this account of her work which mirror what you do.

- Do you agree that the terms play and work can be used interchangeably?

- Montessori laid great emphasis on independence. In what ways do you support children's independence?

Susan Isaacs

PROFILE

Susan Isaacs won a reputation for her practical work with young children and the down-to-earth approach with which she gave confidence to parents and practitioners. She wrote academic books on the psychology of childhood and established the Malting House School in Cambridge. She was the first director of the Department of Child Development at London University.

KEY DATES

1885	Born (Susan Fairhurst) in Lancashire
1913-14	Lecturer in psychology, Darlington Training College
1916-33	Tutor in psychology, University of London
1921	Assistant editor of the British Journal of Psychology
1922	Marries Nathan Isaacs
1924-27	Principal of Malting House School, Cambridge
1933-43	Head of Department of Child Development, University of London, Institute of Education
1948	Awarded CBE for services to education in January. Dies in October

LINKS

Froebel
Dewey
Montessori
Piaget
Freud

Her life

Susan Isaacs (nee Fairhurst) was born in the village of Bromley Cross near Bolton in Lancashire, in 1885. She was the ninth child of William and Miriam Fairhurst. Her father was a lay preacher in the Methodist church as well as a journalist. Her mother became ill shortly after the birth of her last child, Alice, and died when Susan was six years old. Her father had employed a nurse to care for his wife during her long illness and after his wife's death he married her.

As she was growing up, Susan Isaacs was particularly influenced by her brother, Enoch, who introduced her to philosophy. She became agnostic

which led to a rift between her and her father for some years, and she also became interested in music and politics. She left school early – before she was fifteen –and became a nursery governess abroad. She then returned to work in a small private school in Bolton but soon realised that she would not get far without formal training. Isaacs persuaded her father to allow her to take a training course for non-graduates, but her tutors recognised her ability and asked her to consider taking a degree. To be eligible, she had to learn Greek and German, which astonishingly she managed in just three months. Isaacs gained a first class honours degree in philosophy at Manchester. This won her a postgraduate scholarship at Newnham College, Cambridge, where she studied psychology.

Her first job was as a lecturer in infant education at Darlington Training College. During this time she married a former fellow student at Manchester, William Brierley, a botanist. The marriage was dissolved after five years. In 1922, she married Nathan Isaacs. She began her medical training to become a psychoanalyst and passed her preliminary examinations. She became associated with the work of the National Institute of Industrial Psychology and the British Psychological Society, writing the book *Introduction to Psychology*.

In 1924 Isaacs responded to a newspaper advertisement for someone to set up an educational experiment. Geoffrey Pyke and his wife, Margaret, wanted to establish a small school, catering for up to 20 children, where new teaching ideas could be tried. Isaacs was employed to set up and run the school, which was for children from two and a half to seven. One of the pupils was David Pyke, the only son of Geoffrey and Margaret.

Isaacs stayed at the school for four years and spent the next few years writing up her observations and records. She became attached to her pupils and maintained an interest in them for many years. There are suggestions that she left the Malting House when money became an issue and that she disagreed with Pyke's idiosyncratic views on language development.

Six years later Isaacs was appointed head of the new Department of Child Development at the University of London's Institute of Education. In 1935, she was diagnosed with cancer but she continued to work. With the outbreak of war in 1939, Susan Isaacs became involved once more directly with children. She moved back to Cambridge and started work on a research project studying 86 evacuees and their carers. In January 1948 she was awarded the CBE for her services to education. She died in October that year.

Her writing

Following the publication of her *Introduction to Psychology*, Susan Isaacs began writing about education and children's development in 1916 with an article in a journal called *Parents' Review*. Over the next 30 years she

Play adds to the child's knowledge of the world

wrote many papers and books for academic audiences, but she also continued to write for parents. She wrote for *Nursery World* from 1929 to 1936, under the pen-name of Ursula Wise. Much of her work drew on her experiences at Malting House, where she had kept detailed records and observations. Some of her best known publications include:

Books for parents
- *The Nursery Years* (Routledge, 1929). This book is considered by many to be Isaacs' best book.

- *The Children We Teach* (University of London Press, 1932)

Books based on her work at the Malting House School
- *Intellectual Growth in Young Children* (Routledge, 1930)

- *Social Development of Young Children* (Routledge, 1933)

Studies based on further practical work
- *The Educational Guidance of the School Child* (1936)

- *The Cambridge Evacuation Survey* (1941)

Her theory

Isaacs' philosophy was based on Froebel's notion of learning by doing and inspired by John Dewey's ideas about social interaction and supporting children's interests. The Malting House School exemplified Dewey's belief that education is about living and not simply a preparation for it. She believed that free, unfettered play was of great importance to young children. She wrote[1]:

'Through play... he (sic) adds to his knowledge of the world... No experimental scientist has a greater thirst for new facts than an ordinary healthy active child. Not all his play, however is directed to exploring the physical world or practising new skills. Much of it is social in direction, and belongs to the world of phantasy. He plays at being father and mother, the new baby sister, the policeman, the soldier; at going for a journey, at going to bed and getting up, and all the things which he sees grown-ups doing. Here also his play makes it easier for him to fit himself into his social world. When he becomes the father and the mother, he wins an imaginative insight into their attitude to him, and some little understanding of their sayings and doings; and momentarily feels

their powers and great gifts (as they seem to him) as his own. All the things he may not do and cannot be in real life, he is able to do and be in this play world...'.

Susan Isaacs' interest in psychoanalysis led her to explore the importance of children's emotional development, of which for her play was a part. She gave evidence for the government *Report on Infant and Nursery Schools* in 1933 (Hadow). This extract from her evidence[2] gives a flavour of the kind of nursery Susan Isaacs believed best supported young children's development:

'Quiet, positive encouragement, showing the child what to do and how to do it, is far more effective than scolding or punishment, or emphasis on what he (sic) should not do. Successes should be emphasised; failures should be minimised; and above all any feeling of shame or hostility should be avoided.'

Putting the theory into practice

The school which Isaacs was employed to set up in 1924, the Malting House School, placed an emphasis on children's curiosity, their emotional needs and on the importance of language. In establishing it, Isaacs was able to draw both on her interest in philosophy and in psychoanalysis. The school attracted many critics as well as those attracted to its liberal educational ideas. Geoffrey Pyke, her employer, wanted to teach his son himself but his travels made that impractical. He believed children's minds should be set free so they could observe and draw their own conclusions. He believed in learning through discovery rather than adult-led instruction. His friend, Professor John Cohen, quotes Pyke as saying[3]:

'The fundamental principle we should follow in dealing with children is to treat every child as a distinguished foreign visitor who knows little or nothing of our language or customs. If we invited a distinguished stranger to tea and he spilled his cup on the best table cloth or consumed more than his share of cake, we should not upbraid him and send him out of the room. We should hasten to reassure him that all was well. One rude remark from the host would drive the visitor from the room, never to be seen again. But we address children constantly in the rudest fashion and yet expect them to behave as models of politeness. If the principle suggested is to prove effective, there must be no exceptions. One rude remark to the child would give the game away.'

Evelyn Lawrence, a contemporary of Susan Isaacs, identifies the three most interesting things about Malting House School as:

- the emphasis on curiosity and finding out;

- the use and development of language to promote thinking; and

- the attention paid to children's emotional needs.

Susan Isaacs believed in the importance of play. She argued that, with gentle guidance, children could make sense of the world for themselves.

She was especially sensitive to the emotional needs of children and taught that adults should never be sarcastic towards children, or break promises made to them. Children's fantasies should not be curbed and their questions should be answered seriously and respectfully.

Lawrence saw advantages for children in the free environment which Isaacs created. She said that it allowed adults to really get to know children; that their emotions were not hidden and that children learned to regulate their own behaviour within the social group, rather than relying on adults to make decisions for them. Like Dewey, observation was the cornerstone of Isaacs' work with children. Everything that happened was recorded in meticulous detail and this together with her overall approach to education allowed her to reflect on children's learning. Isaacs argued that the characteristics of young children – the restlessness, the constant questioning and the ways in which they run and climb and dig and explore – are essential elements of childhood – "the glory of the human child, his human heritage... the representatives in him of human adventurousness and hard-won wisdom, and the means by which he in his turn will lay hold of knolwedge and skill, and add to them"[1].

What does practice look like?

Evelyn Lawrence describes the happiness of the children as her first impression of the Malting House School: 'I have never seen so much pleased concentration, so many shrieks and gurgles and jumpings for joy as here'[2]. There was no fixed curriculum – children followed their interests.

Inside, there was a piano, a rest gallery with mattresses and rugs, huge amounts of art and craft materials, easels and small tables and chairs (a legacy of the influence of Maria Montessori). There was a real typewriter – and every imaginable kind of equipment from dressing-up clothes to magnifying glasses. The equipment enabled children to follow their interests and Isaacs also encouraged children's curiosity to be rooted in real life. Where interests demanded posting letters, additional purchases or visits, these activities became part of the children's experiences.

Exciting as the indoor environment was, the outdoor area was even more enticing. The school room opened onto a garden, where there was a summer house, sand pit, see-saw (built to Pyke's design) and hutches for rabbits and guinea pigs. There were chickens and cats, snakes and even a salamander. Each child had a little garden plot to cultivate and there were fruit trees. The school had the first climbing frame seen in this country – but children were also encouraged to climb trees and even to climb the summerhouse (though only one at a time). Children were allowed to use double-handed tree saws to encourage co-operation and a range of other tools were available. Risk was a theme in provision – probably as part of the emotional freedom. Children were allowed to light bonfires and use ladders. Isaacs believed that what she termed children's "complete immunity" to risk came about because in exploring their environment freely they developed "skill and poise".

Her influence

Isaacs' writings had a huge impact on the educational world of the late 1920s and 1930s. Isaacs said that her ideas were based on those of Froebel and Dewey but she made those ideas accessible in the way she interpreted and explained them. The combination of curricular ideas with psychoanalytical influences made a major contribution to this field. The rigour which she brought to her work at the Institute of Education in London gave early childhood education a place in academic circles. She visited Piaget's research centre in Geneva and hosted his visit to the Malting House School in 1927. She was critical of some of Piaget's work, believing that he placed too little emphasis on the social and emotional aspects of learning. She disagreed with his view of children's development as a staged process. For her, children's development differed from adults only in the amount of experience that they had to draw on. She also challenged Montessori's view of education – replacing the structure with large amounts of freedom to play imaginatively.

Her advice to parents was well received and encouraged parents (and practitioners) to look at children's motives and drives rather than repressing their natural behaviour. In the present day, Isaacs has "changed our way of seeing children"[4]. From her comes the idea of children as voracious learners. The freedom given to them has influenced outdoor provision. Although her zest for providing opportunities for children to learn to manage risk is not widely practised, her example offers a continuing example of what is possible.

Common criticisms of her theory

Isaacs' theories were based on her experiences with a small group of advantaged children. There were usually only ten children at the Malting House School at any one time. The children came from rich, academic families and were mostly boys, who were considered bright and with a high incidence of difficult or challenging behaviour. Isaacs herself agonised about the relative demands of freedom and the need to protect children from others' aggression. She was not always successful in this.

One of Isaacs' biographers, Smith[1] has suggested that the freedom she advocated for children was not well-liked amongst parents, suggesting that for working-class families vocational training was the priority. Amongst middle class parents the requirements for university entrance seemed more pressing. Some of Isaacs' contemporaries thought that it would be unhelpful to educate working class children to think. They linked this view to Dewey's emphasis on democracy – of which they were equally critical.

Somewhat surprisingly, Isaacs' view of intelligence was that it was fixed rather than that it could be developed. This view was common at the time and was shared with her colleague at London University, Cyril Burt. He was disgraced shortly after his death for having falsified experiments to suggest that intelligence was a product of nature rather than nurture.

POINTS FOR REFLECTION

○ In what ways do you encourage children to learn to manage risk in their play?

○ What elements of Isaacs' outdoor provision would you like to add to your own?

○ Think about situations you have observed where children's freedom has undermined another child's freedom. How have you managed the situation?

Risk-taking was encouraged

Jean Piaget

PROFILE

The work of Jean Piaget has dominated thinking about the nature of children's learning since the 1960s. His theories continue to be both criticised and admired, and to shape subsequent theories of learning.

KEY DATES

1896	Born at Neuchatel, Switzerland
1918	Becomes a Doctor of Natural Sciences
1921	Becomes Director of Studies at Jean-Jacques Rousseau Institute, Geneva
1923	Marries Valentine Chatenay
1923	Becomes Professor of Psychology, Sociology and Philosophical Sciences, University of Neuchatel
1925	Daughter, Jacqueline, born
1927	Daughter, Lucienne, born
1929	Becomes Professor of Child Psychology, University of Geneva
1930	Son, Laurent, born
1933	Becomes Director of Institute for Educational Sciences, University of Geneva
1938	Becomes Director of Psychology and Sociology, University of Lausanne
1940	Becomes Director of Experimental Psychology, University of Geneva
1971	Made Professor Emeritus, University of Geneva
1980	Dies on 16 September, in Geneva

LINKS

Isaacs
Vygotsky
Donaldson
Gardner

His life

Jean Piaget was born in Neuchatel in Switzerland in August 1896. At the age of ten he published his first scientific paper – an observation of an albino sparrow he had discovered near his home. An after-school job at the local natural history museum led him to write a series of articles on molluscs and he was invited to become a curator at a museum in Geneva. However, he declined because he wanted to continue his secondary education.

He chose to study zoology at the University of Neuchatel and completed his doctorate in 1918. It was his godfather, the Swiss scholar Samuel Cornut, who introduced him to philosophy and epistemology (which is the theory of knowledge). Even at this young age, he began to publish articles about the epistemological issues that were to occupy him for life.

After graduating, Piaget became interested in psychology, which was still a new science. He went to Zurich where he studied under Carl Jung and Eugen Bleuler, then to the Sorbonne, in Paris, for two years. It was here that he administered reading tests to schoolchildren and worked with Alfred Binet who was devising intelligence tests. Piaget became bored with counting the number of correct answers, but fascinated by his discovery that children of the same age often gave the same incorrect answers. This led him to explore the development of the reasoning process. His observations led him to believe that there were consistent measurable differences in the nature of reasoning at different ages.

In 1921, he returned to Switzerland where he was appointed Director of the Jean-Jacques Rousseau Institute in Geneva. Two years later, Piaget married and returned to his home town of Neuchatel, becoming Professor of Psychology, Sociology and Philosophical Sciences at his old university. Piaget observed and recorded the development of all three of his children. This shaped his understanding and theories about the ways in which children construct knowledge. Piaget moved back to Geneva in 1929, remaining there until his death in 1980.

His writing

Piaget wrote many books and articles. In many of them, he continued the work started in Paris, developing his theory that the mind of the child evolves through a series of pre-determined stages to adulthood. His books are not easy to read but two of the most influential are:

- *The Psychology of Intelligence* (Routledge Classics, 2001). First published as *La Psychologie de l'intelligence* in 1947. (First published in English in 1950)

- *The Language and Thought of the Child* (Routledge Classics, 2002). First published as *Le langage et la pensee chez l'enfant* in 1923. (First published in English in 1926)

Piaget developed theories about children's understanding of conservation of matter

His theory

Piaget's theories are complex. Five important aspects of his theories in relation to young children's learning and development are outlined below:

Stages of development

Piaget's contemporary, Freud, also identified staged development. While Freud focused on emotional and sexual development, Piaget was interested in intellectual development. Piaget saw the child as constantly constructing and re-constructing reality – achieving increased understanding by integrating simple concepts into more complex ones at each stage of development. He argued that there was a natural sequence for the development of thought governed by what he termed 'genetic epistemology'. It was not enough to teach ideas by simple reinforcement or practice – the child had to be at a particular stage of development to be able to learn new concepts. Piaget identified four stages in that process, from birth through to adulthood:

Sensorimotor stage

Piaget described the first two years of a child's life as the sensorimotor stage when babies' and toddlers' knowledge and understanding are chiefly drawn from physical action and their senses – sight, sound, taste, touch and smell. He suggested that throughout this stage children remain egocentric but become aware of object permanence (see below).

Preoperational stage

From the age of two to around six or seven years of age, children learn to manipulate the environment and to represent objects by words, which supports play with ideas. Logic rests on incomplete knowledge – children of this age may, for example, explain the wind by claiming that trees make it.

Concrete operational stage

In the third stage, from about seven to eleven years of age, logical thought develops, with the child emphasising classification or categorisation by similarity and difference. Logic is normally only applied to things that are tangible or can be seen.

Formal operations stage

The fourth and final stage begins at around the age of twelve and continues through into adulthood. Piaget claimed that this stage was characterised by orderly thinking and mastery of logical thought.

A rich and varied experience was valued

Children can manipulate abstract ideas, make hypotheses and see the implications of their thinking and that of others.

Equilibrium, accommodation and assimilation

One of Piaget's many ideas is auto-regulation or equilibrium. When we take in new information – through the feel of something, sounds, sights or smells – in Piaget's terms we assimilate the information. We are aware of the new sensation or experience but simply put the information alongside our existing ideas. Sooner or later something happens which causes us to call our new idea into question, we experience some discomfort or disequilibrium which causes us to rethink the idea we had assimilated. The rethinking is known as accommodation – we have to adjust or re-organise our thinking in order to restore equilibrium – feeling comfortable with our thinking.

An example of this might be when a young child picks up a piece of paper and the toy which was wrapped up inside it falls out, making a sound. The baby will at first assimilate the idea that paper makes a clunking sound – testing out the idea on several pieces of paper. Over time he or she begins to realise that not all paper makes that particular sound, disequilibrium follows and will lead to an accommodation of the view that paper can only produce that particular sound in certain circumstances. Piaget used the term schema to describe the mental representations that develop as children have new experiences and put new ideas and abilities together. This term was later used by Chris Athey (see page 67). It has many meanings but during the past 20 years has come to have a specific meaning in the education of young children.

Object permanence

Piaget watched his daughter, Jacqueline, at the age of seven months

trying to catch a toy duck on her quilt. She reached to grasp the toy but it slid away from her between the folds. Although she followed the movement with her eyes, as soon as the duck disappeared, she no longer looked for it. Some months later, Piaget put a coin in his hand and hid his hand under the bed cover. When he pulled his hand out from under the cover, his daughter opened it to find the coin. Because it was not there she immediately looked under the cover and found it. These observations led to the formation of Piaget's theory of object permanence – the realisation that objects have their own existence, independent of our perception of them.

Egocentrism

After observing his own children, Piaget carried out a series of experiments with young children. In one of the experiments, he showed children in the pre-operational stage of development a model of three distinctive mountains. A small doll was moved about on the model. Children were shown a series of photographs of the mountains and asked to identify which of the pictures showed what the doll would be able to see from various viewpoints. Most of the children were unable to select the appropriate photograph, choosing instead the one which gave their own point of view. Piaget described this as egocentrism. (To see a similar task being carried out by a child go to www.youtube.com/watch?v=P7w8YxDbdiA)

Conservation

Piaget also carried out a series of conservation task experiments with children under seven years of age. In these experiments, children might be presented with two balls of Plasticene weighing the same. One ball would be flattened and the children asked to predict whether the two lumps would now weigh the same or different. Similarly they might be presented with two identical short, fat beakers of liquid. One would be poured into a tall thin container and, again, children would be asked to say whether the two amounts of liquid were still the same or whether they were different. In another, similar experiment, two rows of buttons were compared before and after one row had been spread out so that it was longer. In these experiments, younger children tended to assume that the amounts had changed, while as they grew older they realised that the amounts stayed the same, whether or not their visual perception supported this view. (To see a similar task being carried out by a child go to www.youtube.com/watch?v=whT6w2jrWbA)

Putting the theory into practice

Piaget's theories have practical implications:

- New ideas and knowledge should be presented at a level and style consistent with the child's current mode of thought. Piaget suggested that there were limitations to the logical thought of young children.

- Teaching should be matched to the needs of individuals. Children should be presented with moderately novel situations or experiences to trigger assimilation and accommodation. Open-ended questions can support this process.

- Learning is supported by action. Children need to experiment actively with materials and to experience things in the real world to develop thought.

- Children need to have control over their learning – learning how to find out and constructing knowledge for themselves. This requires open-ended activities.

- Children require long, uninterrupted periods of play and exploration.

- Observation of what children do and say can and should inform understanding of children's intellectual development – this will tell adults where support is needed.

What does practice look like?

Practice shaped by Piagetian theory places a strong emphasis on experience. So, in early childhood there will be a wide range of activities for children to engage in, over extended periods of time. Children are unlikely to be brought together in large groups but small interest-led groups will emerge – offering adult interaction to a small number of children at a time while other children are free to pursue their explorations.

Since much of Piaget's work focuses on children making sense of their world, opportunities for real life experiences are key. Visits to farms and factories, taking trips to stations or markets are seen as providing children with experiences that feed their thinking and understanding, as are activities such as cooking or caring for animals in the classroom. Activities that are open-ended are seen as being of more value than those that have pre-determined outcomes. For example, making Christmas cards should involve opportunities for free use of glitter, shiny paper and tinsel rather than a template for a snowman and provision simply of cotton wool.

Adults' questioning of children should also be open-ended – rather than questions which have a single answer, questions that begin with "what do you think...?" allow space for children to think and develop curiosity. Challenging questions (which generally do not have factual answers) can induce the disequilibrium which leads to new thinking or in other words make children unsure about what to think and seek to resolve the problem.

Staged theory means that children are not pressed to take on new learning until they are deemed ready. It is likely that opportunities for play with water containers of different shape, sizes and capacities; or with heavy and light objects which challenge the idea that big=heavy or small=light help children to become ready for further learning.

Since young children are seen by Piaget as being egocentric there will be an emphasis on resources which promote social interaction. For example, carts which require cooperation between children maybe more in evidence than bikes for individuals.

His influence

It would be difficult to over-state Piaget's influence. Even his critics have acknowledged the importance of his work and the way in which it shaped subsequent ideas. His major achievements were in creating a sense of curiosity about the ways in which children learn – his interest was primarily in how children learn as opposed to what or when they might learn it. Piaget's theories dominated developmental psychology in the 1960s and 70s. His theories were covered in teacher training and were influential in the education of young children. Many theorists – such as Susan Isaacs, Jerome Bruner and Margaret Donaldson – studied with him over many decades and his influence continues to be felt. Seymour Papert (who developed the computer language, Logo) described Piaget as having 'found the secrets of human learning and knowledge hidden behind the cute and seemingly illogical notions of children' while Albert Einstein said that Piaget's work was 'a discovery so simple that only a genius could have thought of it'. [2]

The detailed diaries which Piaget and his wife kept of the development of their three children have been highly influential. The diaries record minute by minute behaviours of the children even as tiny babies. "There have been baby diaries before and since, but there is nothing like the Piaget diaries"[3]. These diaries have undoubtedly influenced understanding amongst early years practitioners of the practical value of observation.

Common criticisms of Piaget's theories

Piaget is said to be one of the most frequently mentioned and least understood developmental psychologists. Criticisms of his work include:

Active learning involves play and experience

- too much emphasis on logic and mathematical thinking, at the expense of consideration of the role of feelings;

- play and imagination were seen as leading children to mature thought rather than having a long-term intrinsic role in learning;

- the findings from both the observations of his own children and his experiments are over-generalised. His results are criticised for their reliance on data collected from a small number of white, privileged Swiss children;

- the stages offer a snapshot of development. Observations could be interpreted to show continuous development as opposed to the quantitative shifts in thinking which Piaget described;

- insufficient emphasis on the importance of social and emotional aspects of thought;

- some experiments have shown that when what we ask children to do, or respond to, makes 'human sense'[1] – they are able to take another's point of view and to conserve quantities. When a naughty child hiding from a policeman is substituted for mountains or when a naughty teddy bear spreads out the row of buttons, children are more likely to give the correct answers;

- Piaget's description of 'the child' is often criticised as being essentially male – marginalising female behaviour.

GLOSSARY

Accommodation: rethinking which occurs as learners reconcile old and new learning.

Assimilation: the process by which learners take in new information, but at this stage it exists alongside old learning.

Conservation: understanding that two similar amounts or quantities remain the same even though their appearance may have changed.

Disequilibrium: the state that exists when new learning has been assimilated, but not accommodated.

Egocentrism: unable to take another's point of view.

Equilibrium: the state that exists when new information has simply been accommodated.

Object permanence: realisation that objects exist in their own right and that the fact that we cannot see them does not mean that they do not exist.

Schemas: repeated patterns of behaviour which reflect children's preferred modes of exploration.

Stage theory: an approach which claims that there are distinct stages through which all children pass in a particular order, according to a timetable set by nature.

POINTS FOR REFLECTION

- What evidence have you seen of Piaget's influence on practice in the early years?

- Do you think that there are distinct stages of development or is development simply one long continuum?

- Are young children egocentric as Piaget described them or do they show signs of being able to take someone else's point of view?

Piaget believed that young children were egocentric

Lev Vygotsky

PROFILE

Lev Vygotsky was a Soviet psychologist whose book, *Thought and Language*, has become a classic text in university courses on psycholinguistics. He is best known for his emphasis on the way in which children's cultural and social context influences their development. Although he died young and his work was not translated into English until the second half of the twentieth century, he has had a strong influence on the development of current educational theories.

KEY DATES

1896	Born in Orsha, Belarus
1913-1917	Studies at Moscow University
1919	Becomes ill with tuberculosis
1924	Research fellow, Moscow Institute of Psychology
1934	Dies

LINKS

Piaget
Bandura
Bruner
Malaguzzi

Learning with more experienced others

His life

Lev Vygotsky was born in 1896 in Orsha, Belarus. His family were middle-class Jews – his father a bank manager and local philanthropist. As a child, he studied with a private tutor for many years until he was enrolled in a Jewish grammar school which prepared pupils for entrance to university. As a teenager, Vygotsky was an intellectual with a wide range of interests, especially in philosophy and history, including Jewish culture. He graduated from school with honours. At his parents' insistence he applied to the Medical School of Moscow University. Only 3% of the university's intake were Jewish and places were allocated through a draw. Vygotsky gained a place and was at the university from 1913 to 1917. He switched from medicine to law during his first term.

At the same time, he enrolled at the private Shaniavsky University where he studied history, literature and philosophy. He became interested in a wide range of subjects, including the theatre, and was an aspiring literary critic. After graduating, Vygotsky went to Gomel, where his parents lived, and took a job teaching literature in the provincial school. It was there that his health began to deteriorate. He was 23.

He did not enjoy teaching in the school but found a job at a local teachers' training college where he lectured in psychology. He became involved in the education of children with physical disabilities. In 1924, at the second Psychoneural Congress in Leningrad, Vygotsky gave a talk on the relationship between conditioned reflexes and the conscious behaviour of humans. His work so impressed his audience that, at the age of 28, Vygotsky was invited to become a research fellow at the Moscow Institute of Psychology.

During his time in Moscow, Vygotsky wrote about 100 books and papers. He read and reflected on the work of Freud and Piaget. He travelled in Europe during the 1920s and was influenced by a range of writers, including Charlotte Buhler who studied the development of language in babies and children. Vygotsky was also involved in applied research. His experimental studies in educational psychology were developed in his work with mentally and physically disabled children and more generally in the field of psychopathology.

The zone of proximal development is bridged by working with those who are more experienced

His writing

Vygotsky was a prolific writer. Much of his work has not been translated into English but some books have been published in a range of translations and editions. His best known and most influential are:

- *Thought and Language* (published in 1962 by MIT Press)

- *Mind in Society* (published in 1978 by Harvard University Press, edited by M Cole et al.)

His theory

For Vygotsky, the child was not egocentric (as Piaget suggested) but social; not even logical or even illogical (again as Piaget believed) but striving to make sense of the world through communicating. It may be argued that the communist culture within which Vygotsky lived led him to value the collective rather than the individual and to develop theories which focused on the social and environmental aspects of development. The focus of his theory included three key elements, namely: play, language, and socio-cultural aspects.

Play

One important aspect of Vygotsky's theory was play. He famously argued that in their play children perform at a higher level than in other real-life contexts. Play therefore gives children an opportunity to identify solutions to problems and to develop an understanding of rules. Some rules are identified by children as they play but others are dictated by what they believe to be the rules under which people operate. Mums cook, grannies don't dance and so on.

Communication, language and thought

Vygotsky emphasised the significant role that language plays in the development of abstract thought. He stressed the importance of the labelling process in the formulation of concepts. He believed that children's language was social in origin because it arose in interaction between the child and others. In other words, the child's language both results from and is part of social interaction.

He saw the experience of talking with adults about familiar everyday experiences as crucial, not only for building up knowledge of language but also for an awareness of particular ways of thinking and interpreting their own experiences. The very naming of particular attributes, he thought, helped concepts to form. This contrasts with Piaget's view that the use of relevant language follows the development of a concept. Vygotsky believed that talking is necessary to clarify important points but also that talking with others helps us to learn more about communication. Children solve practical tasks with the help of speech, as well as with their eyes and hands. The idea that children observe conversation and that it is the unity of perception, speech and action which leads them to make sense of situations was important in Vygotsky's thinking. Children do not simply react to the words that are used but interpret the context, facial expression, and body language to understand meaning.

Young children also talk to themselves. They use language as a tool for regulating or guiding their actions. An example of this might be the toddler declaring 'up step' as they climb a flight of stairs or a four-year-old creating a story as they draw or paint. Language usually becomes internalised by the age of seven, except where tasks are difficult – adults often talk to themselves through a difficult task or read instructions out loud.

Socio-cultural influences

Arguably, the best known aspect of Vygotsky's thinking is the 'zone of proximal development'. This can best be described as the gap between what a child can do alone and what they can do with the help of someone more skilled or experienced, who could be an adult or another child. Vygotsky argued that the capacity to learn through instruction was a fundamental feature of human intelligence. Where adults help a child to learn, they are fostering the development of knowledge and ability.

While Piaget believed that learning was dependent on the child's readiness to learn, for Vygotsky, the key factors were not only the child's existing knowledge or understanding but also their ability to

What does practice look like?

No theory is more widely quoted than Zone of Proximal Development (ZPD). Practitioners throughout the English-speaking world refer to the idea of scaffolding or ZPD – often without fully understanding what is involved. Some scaffolding occurs naturally or intuitively as when parents support children's language development – using a limited vocabulary and structure until they are clear that the child can cope with more complex forms. This occurs either when the parent uses a complex form by mistake or when the child uses it and appears to understand what he or she is saying. It may also occur when adults offer unfamiliar words or language structures and repeat in different ways, with different emphases to ensure that the child understands.

It has been suggested[1] that scaffolding by adults or by more experienced children (sometimes referred to as more knowledgeable others or MKOs) involves:

- clear purpose;

- appropriate level of challenge – neither too hard or too simple;

- modelling ideas, actions or language which the child can imitate and use in similar situations independently;

- collaboration – opportunities for the learner to collaborate wherever possible is essential to effective scaffolding;

- internalisation – support is gradually withdrawn as the learner (or apprentice) acts increasingly independently.

This process is strengthened where two adults or 'paired pedagogues' work side by side – one acting as the expert and the other modelling questioning which will extend knowledge and understanding.

Social and cultural aspects of practice

Interaction with others may produce a kind of mental conflict which in turn produces new learning. Nan's cat is called Charlie – but suddenly they are introduced to the idea that cats may have any number of different names. Fifty four may be a familiar bus number but it might also be someone else's door number – or even their age! A similar conflict can arise as children are introduced to different resources – large objects are usually heavy but what about this tiny parcel that is very heavy? Through these interactions children construct new understandings and conceptual insights.

The cultural tools or tools for thinking which we use are part of everyday practice but are often overlooked. Numbers and diagrams are examples of things we use to help us think – but we may forget that poetry, stories, dance, music, art and maps are also cultural tools. All over the world tools for thinking are used and developed according to the cultural needs of society. Bruner suggests that cultural tools "provide a means for turning around upon one's thoughts, for seeing them in a new light"[2].

Perhaps the best-known example of tools for thinking in action occurs in Reggio Emilia. Reggio practitioners refer to tools for thinking as the Hundred Languages of Childhood. Children are encouraged to represent ideas in a range of different media. Drawing, then painting, then modelling, then acting out the same object or event transforms the child's understanding of it. Transformation is a vital element of Vygotsky's theory and occurs as children internalise concepts and ideas. It could be argued that this process accounts for children's liking for transformers – a toy that mirrors the internal process.

Rogoff[3] offers a summary of the factors that practice built on Vygotsky's theory would include. She suggests that collaboration would be key; learning based on adults' observation of children's interests and environment; adults guiding children's learning by working closely with them; and opportunities to work in mixed age groups.

learn with help. Two children may have similar levels of competence but different levels of success because of their differing abilities to benefit from the help or instruction given them by adults. For this reason, he objected to measuring children's abilities through intelligence tests, believing that what could be observed about how the child went about a task could reveal as much as the score of any test.

Vygotsky rated children's interactions between themselves as important. In his view, interaction benefits a child when they are helped by another child who knows more about the task. The more knowledgeable child benefits too, as the process of making their ideas more explicit renders the grasp of what they know clearer and more objective.

For Vygotsky, social and cognitive development work together. While Piaget believed that knowledge comes from personal experience, Vygotsky emphasised the importance of families, communities and other children. Vygotsky saw language as one of a range of cultural tools or tools for thinking, which we learn from others and use with others in thinking and learning. Other such tools are numbers, signs, notations, plans and diagrams.

Putting the theory into practice

In his short life, Vygotsky did little to put his theory into practice. However, other theorists have been keen to do so. The notion of the zone of proximal development (ZPD) emphasises the importance of what has been called 'scaffolding' – a term developed by Bruner. This relies on careful observation of what children can do and planning a curriculum which challenges their current capability.

Like Piaget, Vygotsky emphasised the way in which knowledge and understanding are constructed by the learner from their experiences. This is known as constructivist theory. Unlike Piaget, however, who saw experience as personal, Vygotsky emphasised the social components of experience. His theory underlined the contribution to learning made by others, and is known as a social constructivist view. It has been associated with an apprenticeship approach where the learner learns from someone more experienced or competent. Key ideas in a classroom then become conversation, play and opportunities for children to follow their own interests and ideas.

His influence

Vygotsky's concept of differing zones of proximal development led to important new techniques for diagnosing children's learning needs and the development of teaching techniques to meet them. The idea of matching tasks to children's current competence to scaffold their learning comes directly from his work. His theories changed the way educators think about children's interactions with others, and led to peer tutoring approaches and to apprenticeship views of learning. Schemes encouraging children to read at home with their parents rely on a view that children are apprentice readers.

Vygotsky's ideas balance those of Piaget and helped others build on

and develop new theories from those of Piaget. The work of Bruner, for example, owes much to Vygotsky. American psychologist Barbara Rogoff[4] has developed detailed theories and approaches based on Vygotsky's emphasis on culture and society. Bronfenbrenner, who has been described as "the father of the Head Start program" developed an ecological system of learning which highlights the cultural factors that impact on learning and development.

Common criticisms of his theory

Because Vygotsky died so young, criticisms of his work have not been as detailed or as analytical as those of Piaget's work. His work was not widely known outside Russia for many years after his death. In emphasising the nurture side of learning (the impact of others and the scaffolding they offer to learning), it could be argued that there is not enough emphasis on children's role in their own development – the nature of learning, the role played by the developmental process and the child's own personality. The second criticism concerns Vygotsky's methodologies. Much of his work was not based on empirical evidence but involved untested ideas or hypotheses. Another area of criticism concerns language. It is claimed[1] that in placing so much emphasis on the role of language in learning, Vygotsky "ignores all the implicit knowledge we have of the world which we have never put into words". This links with the view expressed by some critics that Vygotsky's theories are incomplete. If so this is perhaps understandable, given his early death.

GLOSSARY

Apprenticeship approach to learning: children learn by working alongside more expert or experienced others.

Constructivist theory: belief that individuals build up knowledge and understanding through experience.

Cultural tools or tools for thinking: systems or devices used within a culture to support learning and thinking.

Multi-modality: belief that knowledge and understanding are built up through interactions with others.

Transformation: process of changing views by creating changing representations, for example a child makes a car, which becomes a house, which is then transformed into a suitcase and so on.

Zone of proximal development (ZPD): the gap between what a child can do unaided and what he or she can do with support.

POINTS FOR REFLECTION

○ Observe a child at play and identify the transformations that he or she makes.

Burrhus Skinner and behaviourist theories

PROFILE

Burrhus Skinner is probably the best known behaviourist theorist. Skinner applied ideas taken from his work with rats and pigeons to children. His approach is called operant conditioning. He was identified in a 1975 survey as the best-known American scientist of his day.

KEY DATES

1904–1990	Burrhus Skinner (USA)
1849-1936	Ivan Pavlov (Russia)
1874-1949	Edward Thorndike (USA)
1878-1954	John Watson (USA)
1925	Albert Bandura (Canada)

LINKS

Piaget
Vygotsky

Behaviour is shaped by reward

His life

Burrhus Skinner was born in 1904 in Pennsylvania, USA. His father was a lawyer and his mother a housewife. He had one younger brother. At university, he had aspirations to be a writer. He wrote poetry, took courses in Greek, creative writing and drama and became editor of the student newspaper. He also enjoyed painting and music. After graduating, Skinner wrote to the poet Robert Frost, asking for advice about a career. Frost's response led him to apply for a course in psychology at Harvard University. In the late 1920s, Skinner read the work of Ivan Pavlov and John Watson. Their theories later influenced his work.

In 1931 he gained a PhD and became a teacher. He married in 1936 and was to have two daughters. They were later to become the subject of conjecture about the part they had played in his experimental work[1]. During World War II Skinner worked on a secret project training pigeons to maintain the course of missiles – work which also influenced his future experiments.

His writing

Skinner had many books and articles in journals published, from early in his career until he was more than 80 years old. These are some of his more famous works:

- *The Behaviour of Organisms: an experimental analysis* (Prentice Hall, 1938)

- 'The science of learning and the art of teaching' *Harvard Educational Review* 24: 86-97 (1954)

- *Verbal Behaviour* (Appleton-Century-Crofts, 1957)

- 'Teaching machines' *Scientific American* November 1961, pages 91-102

- *Beyond Freedom and Dignity* (Alfred Knopf, 1971)

His theory

Skinner conducted most of his experiments on rodents and pigeons but wrote most of his books about people. His work became widely applied to child development and to work with parents. To him, people and animals are organisms – differing only in the degree of sophistication they bring to a learning situation. Behaviourism is sometimes known as learning theory. A key feature of behaviourist theories is that inner processes such as thinking and feeling have no part to play – that only what the researcher can see, namely actions, is studied.

Learning and development are often portrayed in terms of nature versus nurture. Behaviourism is at the extreme nurture end of this debate –

behaviourists generally believe that all behaviour is learned and that it can be shaped. This shaping process is known as conditioning. Skinner's version is known as operant conditioning – often referred to as instrumental, or even Skinnerian, conditioning. This varies from classical conditioning (see below in section on Ivan Pavlov), which focuses on specific reflex actions. Operant conditioning, on the other hand, is used to modify whole patterns of behaviour. The popular view is that behaviour is shaped by punishment and rewards – that humans act to avoid punishment and gain reward. Skinner emphasised reward which he termed reinforcement. He believed that punishment (as opposed to negative reinforcement) was counter-productive.

Tasks were broken down into small steps, each step reinforced and rewarded as it was learned. Undesirable behaviours or actions take longer to disappear if reinforcement is not consistent. Conversely, Skinner claimed, if rewards are only sometimes given after completing the desired task or action, the behaviour carries on for longer. This is often given as the reason for gambling becoming compulsive. Those who participate are not regularly rewarded, losing at least as frequently as they win.

Skinner also studied what he termed extinction. If rewards for desired actions ceased, then the behaviour ceased as well. Skinner

Behaviourists believed that any child could be brought up to be anything

was particularly interested in how long it took for the behaviour to disappear when not rewarded.

Other behaviourist theories

Ivan Pavlov (1849-1936) was primarily interested in physiology. He was greatly admired by Skinner, particularly for his tireless commitment to his work, and became highly influential in Skinner's research. Pavlov developed the theory of classical conditioning. He discovered that dogs could be trained (or conditioned) to salivate when a bell rang, if feeding was consistently preceded by a bell ringing. Salivating at the sight of food when hungry is a natural response – by pairing a natural response (the reflex action of salivating at the sight of food) with an artificial one (a ringing bell) the two become associated with one another. As in Skinner's operant conditioning, the learned response is conditioned or shaped. In 1904 Pavlov won a Nobel prize for his work.

Edward Thorndike (1874-1949) was a leading educational psychologist in the USA throughout the first half of the twentieth century. He developed the law of effect which suggests that any behaviour leading to a positive consequence will be repeated. Through his experiments with animals he found that repetition improved their ability to solve problems.

John Watson (1878-1954), another behaviourist much admired by Skinner, suggested that operant conditioning is concerned with controlling actions by providing a stimulus after rather than before the action. When reinforcement follows a behaviour, that behaviour is likely to be repeated. In other words, if an adult says 'well done' or gives a child a sweet every time they eat everything on their dinner plate, the child will continue to clear their plate at mealtimes. Watson[2] famously believed that he could shape any child's development saying: 'Give me a dozen healthy infants, well-formed, and my own specified world to bring them up in, and I'll guarantee to take anyone at random and train him to become any type of specialist I might select – doctor, lawyer, artist, merchant-chief, and yes even beggar-man and thief, regardless of his talents, penchants, tendencies, abilities, vocations, and race of his ancestors.'

Albert Bandura (1925-), a Canadian, is known as the father of cognitivists. It is interesting to note that in a 2002 survey, Bandura was rated fourth only behind Skinner, Freud and Piaget amongst the psychologists who were referred to most often.

Bandura's work started as a study of aggression in adolescents, sometimes known as the 'bobo doll studies'. He claimed that aggressive behaviour was learned through observing and imitating role models. Bandura's view is that learning occurs as a result of stimulus (such as the bell) and response (salivating) or the promise of sweets and a clean dinner plate. He claims, however, that reinforcement is most likely to occur as a result of our observation and imitation of other humans, as we try to be like others we like or admire. Bandura's work on social learning theory has been explained as follows: 'Children frequently learn, through observation, the behaviour of both sexes, however, they usually perform only the behaviour appropriate to their own sex because this is what they have been reinforced to do'[3].

Bandura's theory has acted as a bridge between behaviourism and developmental theories. His social learning theory is built on behaviourist theories but also provides a link between the work of Piaget and Vygotsky – with a focus on the impact of social relations on cognition. Unlike behaviourism, Bandura's social behaviourism takes account of the mind, or mental dimensions of human learning, but also recognises that reinforcement is not always immediate and that learning may occur where there is no immediate or apparent reward.

Putting the theory into practice

Behaviourist theory is responsible for teaching methods which focus on the repetition of words and on completing row upon row of sums. Programmed instruction was launched in the 1950s with materials presented in small steps. Behaviourism is most often seen in the teaching of children with special educational needs and in behaviour management. Breaking tasks down into small steps; star charts rewarding children for keeping to rules; withdrawal of privileges when children do not keep to rules – these approaches all come from behaviourism. Similar techniques are often applied to persistently

What does practice look like?

Skinner had a dream that babies could be reared in a totally controlled environment. He devised what has become known as a baby box, or what Skinner himself apparently wanted to call an heir conditioner. Temperature controlled so bedding was unnecessary, padded with special fabric to absorb smells and wetness; no dangerous sharp corners – Skinner believed that the box would help to produce children who would approach the world with total confidence, believing that they could control their surroundings[3].

While that experiment failed, it is easy to find practice based on behaviourist theory because, up to a point, it is widely used in many of our day-to-day interactions. Babies, like Pavlov's dogs, demonstrate classical conditioning when they learn to respond to the sound of their bottle being prepared.

Adults regularly make use of operant conditioning in an effort to help children to 'conform to a culture'[2]. The reward may be a hug for a job well done; going swimming when a bedroom is tidied; a sweet if all the vegetables are eaten and so on. It may be argued that the widespread approach to teaching and learning which relies on learning goals and targeted teaching is a behaviourist approach. This approach is not without critics (see section entitled Common criticisms of behaviourist theories below).

The use of much computer software also relies on behaviourism. In the 1950s, Skinner devised teaching machines. The machine set questions or tasks – if children got the right answer they were rewarded while a wrong answer brought more tasks for further practice.

crying babies – the advice is not to pick babies up when they cry as this will reinforce the crying behaviour.

The influence of behaviourist theories

Just as Freud's work changed society's perception of the unconscious, Pavlov's work, for the first time, showed people connections between human physiology and mental associations. His, and subsequent behaviourist theories, showed too that actions could be shaped and systematically controlled. In addition to this over-arching change in public understanding behaviourism has influenced:

Understanding of language learning

Skinner also wanted to apply behaviourism to language. He believed that all language was learned by reward – for example, when the baby says 'da-da-da' we praise them, but we don't reinforce sounds that we don't recognise or link to other words. Noam Chomsky, an American professor of linguistics, was so opposed to Skinner's views that he developed a theory based on the idea of language development as an innate process. He hypothesised that we are born with a 'language acquisition device' which gives us an inbuilt understanding of language structures. Chomsky's argument, spurred by Skinner's view, stimulated experiment and thinking about language throughout the second half of the twentieth century.

The role of imitation in learning

Bandura's social learning theory has played a role in making practitioners aware of children's need to be offered positive role models in behaviour and conflict resolution, and in habits such as reading and healthy eating.

Research methods

Skinner's experiments provided large amounts of data about learning. This has had a major influence on the way in which attainment and learning outcomes are measured and monitored. This has been described as a "true science of behaviour"[1] with Skinner the first to explore the potential of this approach.

Common criticisms of behaviourist theories

The philosopher Arthur Koestler said 'For the anthropomorphic view of the rat, American psychology substituted a rattomorphic view of man'[1]. This is the most common criticism of behaviourism, that since it focused on animals it is too simplistic a view of human learning and motivation. Rewards can become counter-productive. Studies in which young children were rewarded for drawing pictures, for example, demonstrated that quickly children no longer drew pictures unless they were rewarded.

The development of teaching machines and programmed learning, whether computer based or not, is said to enable children to learn independently. However it is clear that this is untrue since the whole programme has been pre-determined by adults. This underlines a larger criticism of behaviourism – namely that it seeks to control behaviour, infringing human dignity.

Behaviourism ignores the emotional states and complex motives that account for human behaviour. Humans are treated as though they lack mind or soul and consist only of a brain that responds to external stimuli. It does not explain many phenomena in learning. Language learning in young children is a good example of something that cannot be explained through stimulus-response approaches. Small children say things that they have never heard – they make up words, merge words, overgeneralise rules, and so on. They may also fail to say things for which they are rewarded – such as please and thank you! It ignores, too, the way in which patterns of learning can be adapted to new information and the role of thoughtful judgement and reflection in human thinking.

GLOSSARY

Classical conditioning: the subject learns to associate a known action, for example a reflex action, with a new stimulus.

Extinction: when rewards (negative or positive reinforcement) are stopped the learning or behaviour stops over time.

Negative reinforcement: if a rat is feeling an electric current but can find a lever which causes the shock to cease, the ability to avoid the unpleasantness is a negative reinforcer. This is said to be different from punishment which was not used by Skinner.

Intermittent reinforcement: in this case, actions are not reinforced or rewarded every time they occur but rewarded in a random fashion.

Positive reinforcement: pleasant consequences or rewards are used to reward behaviour.

Variable schedules of reinforcement: Skinner discovered that if desired actions were not always rewarded the learning was harder to extinguish.

POINTS FOR REFLECTION

○ Why did Skinner's experiment in using a baby box fail?

○ Have you heard children saying things that they will not have heard other people saying, such as 'goed'? Have you heard them saying things for which they will have been criticised rather than rewarded?

○ Does it matter that much behaviourist research was carried out on animals but was applied to humans?

John Bowlby

PROFILE

John Bowlby's theory of attachment argues that a child's emotional bond to their familial caregiver is a biological response that ensures survival. Bowlby believed that the quality of attachment influences the child's capacity to form trusting relationships throughout life.

KEY DATES

1906–1981	Harry Harlow
1907	Bowlby born
1911–1988	James Robertson
1913–1999	Mary Ainsworth
1969	*Attachment and Loss (Vol 1: Attachment)* is published
1990	Bowlby dies

LINKS

Emotional intelligence
Freud

Bowlby's attachment theory continues to influence policy

His life

John Bowlby was one of six children. Much of his early life was spent in the care of a nanny and at the age of seven he was sent to boarding school. He gained a first degree in psychology at Cambridge but then became a doctor. He subsequently studied psychoanalysis and took up a post at London's Tavistock Clinic.

It was at the end of the Second World War, that Bowlby's work became widely recognised. He was commissioned by the World Health Organisation (WHO) to study the mental health needs of homeless and orphaned children. In his report, *Maternal Care and Mental Health*, he documented the depth of distress in the children he had seen. In his view, this distress could not be explained by the main theories of the time.

Bowlby continued to study how children bond with adults, and their reaction to separation from adults, over the 20 years that followed the publication of the WHO report. In 1969 he published his first book about attachment theory.

His writing

These are the best-known of Bowlby's many books:

- *Child Care and the Growth of Love* (Penguin, 1965)

- *Attachment and Loss Vol 1: Attachment* (Penguin, 1969)

- *Attachment and Loss Vol 2: Separation* (Penguin, 1973)

His theory

In searching for an explanation for the distress of children without a primary caregiver in early childhood Bowlby considered other theories:

- Some theorists, for example, explained the distress as a kind of 'cupboard love'. To meet their physical needs for food, warmth and protection, children attached themselves to an adult who would provide for them. This attachment was secondary to the main purpose of sustenance and protection. However, the depth and manner of young children's responses to separation from adults seemed to Bowlby to go beyond this.

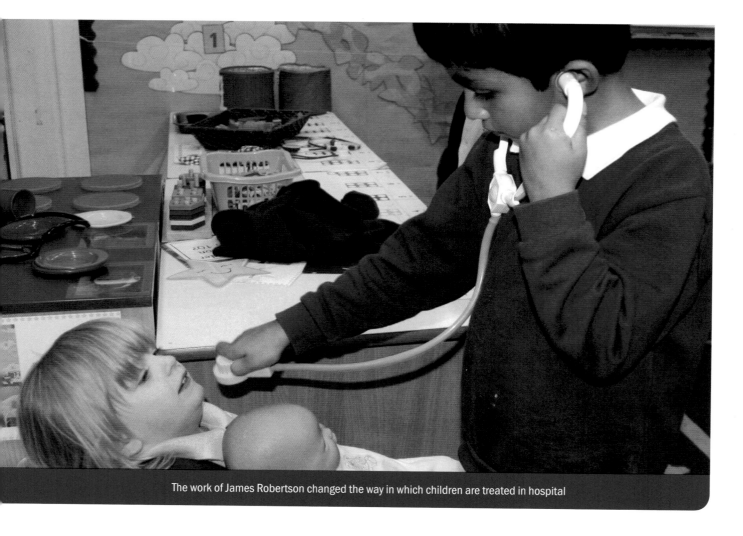

The work of James Robertson changed the way in which children are treated in hospital

Another contemporary theorist was Harry Harlow, an American scientist studying the interactions between rhesus monkeys and their mothers. Harlow found that, when frightened, baby monkeys preferred a comforting mother to a feeding mother. These monkeys were demonstrating that attachment to the 'maternal monkey' mattered in its own right for the sense of comfort and security it provided.

James Robertson, a psychiatric social worker, and Bowlby's student at the Tavistock Clinic, had recorded on film the reactions of young children in short separations from their parents. The children's distress and withdrawal evident in these films had a big impact on public and professional debate about the impact of separation on young children.

Despite the fact that attachment theory has developed and evolved since Bowlby first wrote about it, some striking features remain:

Children show a marked preference for closeness to a small number of adults and these attachments are a normal and universal part of human development.

Babies are born adapted to seek out such attachments not primarily with the aim of being fed and protected but for the feelings of safety and security the attachment brings.

The particular attachment between infant and adult is formed as an interaction in which both play a part.

Attachment behaviour, that is the actions of the infant to bring about physical closeness with an attachment figure, increases when the infant feels frightened or anxious and decreases when the infant feels safe and secure.

As infants mature into adulthood, the need for attachment figures lessens; however, attachment behaviour continues across the life cycle and we find ourselves returning to seek comfort or reassurance from loved ones in times of stress or anxiety.

Our experiences of attachment in infancy (that is how well and how reliably adults respond to infants' feelings of anxiety and dread and expressions of love) influence our closest relationships throughout life.

- There is a sensitive period of some two years for forming these earliest attachments but if early relationships are disrupted, for whatever reason, many other factors come into play to determine how children cope and develop – resilience depends on much more than just the first two or three years of life.

Putting the theory into practice

It is widely assumed that the main positive outcomes of good attachment experiences in the early years are social ones, namely:

- self-confidence;

- efficacy;

- self-esteem;

- the capacity to care for others and to be cared for.

However, these attributes are associated with mastery – the disposition to believe something can be achieved and to keep on trying. Nurseries which value the importance of children's attachments – at home and at nursery – are likely to be ones where links between home and nursery are strong; where children feel that they are known and understood; and where staff know in detail about children's interests and activities.

Many professional staff worry about children becoming too attached to them for fear it will undermine relationships at home. They don't want to set children up for painful feelings of loss when they have to leave nursery or move up a class. They also think that it may lead to favouritism. But children can cope with several close attachments. Attachment is not a fixed quantity in children's lives. More at nursery does not mean less at home. Professional staff, supported by colleagues and managers, are well able to allow children to become attached but to maintain professional boundaries, too. Favouritism is not an inevitable consequence of closeness.

His influence

John Bowlby's work contributed to changes in services for children. After the war, many nurseries cut their hours to part-time. This had the effect of both doubling the number of available places to cater for the boom in births as fathers returned from the war and reducing the number of women seeking employment, creating more job opportunities for men.

James Robertson, Bowlby's student, together with his wife Joyce, produced a film showing the effects of separation from parents on children when hospitalised. This, despite initial resistance from medical staff, shocked the nation and was instrumental in making it possible for parents to stay in hospital with their children.

Bowlby's work led other researchers to try to assess the strength of infants' attachments to adults, mainly their mothers. Most notable of these was Mary Ainsworth. She devised a test to see how infants of

What does practice look like?

The attachment theory was a convenient idea for post-war politicians. During the war, women had done jobs that were now needed for men returning from the war. Many local authorities developed policies supporting the view that children under the age of three should be at home with their mothers. If parents wanted day care for their children then it should be with childminders not nurseries.

Nurseries for children over three that had provided full-time places during the second world war, at the end of the war generally only took children on a part-time basis. This made more places available but it was also argued that children of this age benefited from being at home with their mothers. Many current practices are based on Bowlby's work, including:

- the involvement of parents in their children's learning and development;

- early intervention in families where attachment bonds are not strong;

- requirement for a key person to be identified for each child in an early years setting;

- awareness of the need for supervision so that practitioners are able to support children in forming attachments;

- encouragement for parents to stay with their children if hospitalisation is necessary. Until the 1950s this practice was actively discouraged in the belief that the parents' presence upset the child.

around a year old reacted in different kinds of unusual situations. The test involved a series of short events, starting with the mother and infant settled together in a playroom. The mother left but returned within two or three minutes. The extent to which the infant became anxious at his mother's departure and how quickly and easily she was able to reassure him on her return were taken as measures of the security of his attachment to her.

The categories devised by Ainsworth and subsequent researchers found that most infants (around two thirds of babies tested) were regarded as 'secure' and were easily reassured by the return of their mother. Generally, after seeking and receiving a hug or cuddle, they were happy to carry on playing. The remaining third are often described as follows:

avoidant attachment – the baby's reaction whether to mother or a stranger is similar. The baby does not seek or reject comfort from either.

anxious/resistant attachment – when mother reappears after separation the baby appears angry and is difficult to comfort. In some cases the baby may even seem to prefer the stranger.

anxious-ambivalent – when mother returns, the baby seems not to know what it wants – first seeking reassurance and then rejecting it.

disorganised/disoriented attachment – regarded as the most insecure, babies in this category tend to look away when held and cry unpredictably.

Bowlby's influence can still be seen today. Renewed emphasis on the importance of attachment and bonding has led to increased understanding of the importance of emotional well-being to learning and development. The work of Bowlby and his students, including Robertson and Ainsworth, has informed current thinking about mother and baby interactions[1]. Today such notable researchers as Daniel Stern, Lynne Murray, Colwyn Trevarthen and Dan Siegel, have worked to increase understanding the cognitive benefits of a firm attachment between child and carers. Siegel[2] emphasises the importance of mindsight in allowing humans to judge the emotional state of others. This, in turn, leads to an understanding of intention and to a sense of belonging – key to cognitive development.

Common criticisms of his theory

Critics of Bowlby's work (and that of his followers such as Ainsworth) frequently refer to Bowlbyism. They would emphasise flaws in their theories which include:

- increased difficulty in post-war Britain of obtaining full day care for young children. Feminist writers in particular have criticised the way in which Bowlby's influence on government policy made it more difficult for mothers to work;

- Bowlby's theory was derived from data collected for a section of the population who had been in severely deprived environments such as orphanages. Critics query whether this can be generalised to all children. Bruno Bettelheim (see page 24) rejected Bowlby's claim that a bad home was better than a good institution;

- behaviourist critics believed that expert upbringing, without the complication of attachment, was the key to success.

Bowlby's research methods have been widely criticised. Numbers of children seen in institutions were relatively small and contributing factors, such as abuse, or genetic inheritance were not taken into account. Moreover, children in wartime orphanages were often not only facing the loss of their mother but of home and family.

Mary Ainsworth's work has been criticised as[2] failing to take account of cultural differences, acting as though cultural groups which did not match the responses of American children were somehow failing to attach appropriately. It has been argued that different measures should have been adopted in different cultures.

Bowlby's theory was developed through observation of children experiencing extreme emotional deprivation

GLOSSARY

Attachment: a deep and enduring emotional bond that connects one person to another across time and space, and is characterised by seeking proximity with the attachment figure when upset or worried.

Mindsight: the ability to perceive the mental state of another.

POINTS FOR REFLECTION

○ What is your view about the impact of day care on young children's well-being?

○ What support, if any, are you able to offer to parents experiencing difficulties in bonding with their babies?

○ In your experience, do Mary Ainsworth's categories adequately describe secure and insecure attachments?

Jerome Bruner

PROFILE

Jerome Bruner is a cognitive and developmental psychologist who has been influential in education, bringing together the work of many psychologists, in particular Vygotsky and Piaget. Some dissatisfaction with his own early work led him to focus on the importance of culture in learning and to look at ways of improving education.

KEY DATES

1915	Born in New York City, USA
1959	Chairs joint conference of the National Academy of Sciences and the National Science Foundation in Massachusetts
1970	Joins Oxford University
1980	Oxford Pre-School Research is published
1991	Returns to Harvard University

LINKS

Donaldson
Gardner
Vygotsky
Athey
Piaget
Skinner

Symbolic behaviour develops through learning to visualise

His life

The son of Polish immigrants, Bruner was born in New York in 1915. He received his first degree in psychology in 1937, and subsequently was awarded a PhD in Psychology from Harvard University in 1941. After a period at Oxford University, Bruner returned to Harvard in 1991, still teaching at the age of 98.

Bruner's long life and career has encompassed work in many different areas of psychology. Much of his early work set out to challenge the views of behaviourists such as Skinner, and focused on perception. In 1959 he chaired a prestigious meeting of scientists, psychologists and educators who wanted to improve the quality of scientific education in the USA. The discussions that came from that conference were to lead to his seminal book *The Process of Education*.

Bruner spent some time at Oxford University and led the Oxford Pre-School Research project in the 1980s. He was critical of some aspects of early childhood provision in this country. In the late 1990s, he began to work with the pre-schools of Reggio Emilia and other Italian communities. His work has been increasingly influenced by Vygotsky and the emphasis which he gives to the impact of culture on learning. This has led him to a continued interest in motivation, affect, creativity, intuition – all of which go far beyond and counter to behaviourist theories.

His writing

It would be hard to over-estimate the impact of Bruner's writing. Howard Gardner,[1] a psychologist and educationalist (see page 87), wrote about what he describes as 'Jerome Bruner's remarkable volume', *The Process of Education* as follows:

In the late 1980s, I attended an international conference on education in Paris. One evening I found myself having dinner with half a dozen persons, representing half a dozen different nations, none of whom I had known before. As we spoke, a remarkable fact emerged. All of us had been drawn to a life in education because of our reading, years before, of *The Process of Education*.

Bruner attributed that book's success to the fact that it addressed the concerns of educators about the role of knowledge in an age increasingly over-burdened by knowledge and sources of information. But it is by no means all that he has written and has continued to write well past the age of 90. The books listed below are but a tiny sample of Bruner's work:

- *The Process of Education* (Harvard University Press, 1960)

- *The Process of Education* (Harvard University Press, 1977). This edition has a new introduction by Bruner that attempts to examine the strengths and weaknesses of the original.

- *Play: its Role in Development and Evolution* edited in conjunction with Alison Jolly and Kathy Sylva (Penguin, 1976)

- *Under Five in Britain* (Grant McIntyre, 1980)

- *Child's Talk: Learning to Use Language* (Oxford University Press, 1983)

- *Actual Minds: Possible Worlds* (Harvard University Press, 1986)

- *Making stories: law, literature and life* (Harvard University Press, 2003)

His theory

Bruner has developed many theories, not all of which focus around education and development. *The Process of Education* included ideas which run throughout much of his work:

- 'Knowing how something is put together is worth a thousand facts about it.'

- The child is an active learner and problem-solver, struggling to make sense of the world.

- Intellectual activity is anywhere and everywhere – children are always learning.

- The spiral curriculum, described in Bruner's words[2] as 'any subject can be taught effectively in some intellectually honest form to any child at any stage of development'.

Rich socio-cultural experience supports learning

Bruner developed his theory of the spiral curriculum in the 1960s, when he was thinking of ways in which to reform school curricula. Like Piaget and Vygotsky, Bruner is a constructivist theorist, believing that knowledge is constructed from experience.

In his most recent work, Bruner emphasises the importance of culture, which is a rich source of children's experience. He believes that cultural psychology is the route to understanding people's intentional behaviour. He says that education offers a test bed for developing the discipline of cultural psychology. Bruner has written about the role of culture in education[3]:

> 'It is surely the case that schooling is only one small part of how a culture inducts the young into its canonical ways. Indeed schooling may even be at odds with a culture's other ways of inducting the young into the requirements of communal living. What has become increasingly clear....is that education is not just about conventional school matters like curriculum or standards or testing. What we resolve to do in school only makes sense when considered in the broadest context of what the society intends to accomplish through its educational investment in the young. How one conceives of education, we have finally come to recognize, is a function of how one conceives of culture, and its aims, professed or otherwise...... culture shapes the mind...It provides us with the toolkit by which we construct not only our worlds but our very conception of ourselves and our powers.'

Stages of thinking and learning

Bruner considers the full range of human capacities that are involved in teaching and learning – perception, thought, language, other symbol systems, creativity, intuition, personality and motivation. Most notably, he has developed a model for understanding the way in which children represent experiences and turn them into knowledge. His model identifies three stages or modes:

- the enactive mode, which involves physical action;

- the iconic, in which one thing stands for another, as when a child uses a banana to represent a telephone; and

- the symbolic mode, which suggests that children represent experience through a range of symbolic systems.

While for Piaget, movement between stages was a one-way process, Bruner talks of negotiation and conflict between them. The chosen mode depends on the level of experience. With things that are new to us we are more likely to choose enactive modes of representation or thinking, gradually moving towards symbolic modes as we become more experienced.

This more fluid view of stages of development makes more human sense. Piaget's theory of stage development suggests that once higher levels of thinking are achieved the learner operates solely at that stage. But of course, we are aware that both adults and children vary in the stage at which they operate. As Bruner indicates we can move between different levels of complexity and sophistication of thought.

Scaffolding

Bruner sees education as beginning in infancy and some of his writing has focused on mother–child interactions. He has focused on the importance of the social and playful interactions between adults and babies in supporting the development of language. Bruner has developed Vygotsky's theory of the Zone of Proximal Development (ZPD). In his work he refers to a process of scaffolding as adults helping children to move towards what they intend to achieve from where they are. Bruner describes the starting point as 'incipient intentions' while Vygotsky referred to it as 'the ripening buds'[4].

In refuting Skinner's ideas about how language develops, Noam Chomsky developed an alternative theory of a language acquisition device 'LAD' (see page 58). Bruner rejected both ideas in favour of what he humorously called a language acquisition support system 'LASS', namely a mother. In his view, mothers (or other caregivers) scaffold children's learning of language.

Putting the theory into practice

Bruner attempted to put his theories into practice by creating a curriculum entitled *Man: a course of study*, based on the fundamental questions:

- What is uniquely human about human beings?

- How did they get that way?

- How could they be made more so?

The curriculum drew on the work of contemporary thinkers such as Noam Chomsky and Levi-Strauss and included issues related to communication, tools and media, the social organisation of cultures (art, myth and childrearing practices) and focused on the Inuit and Kalahari bushmen. Although this experiment was by no means wholly successful, the application of Bruner's theory of stages of representation can be seen in the way in which practitioners seek to enable children to represent their ideas and experiences:

- actively through play;

- iconically through building or painting; and

- symbolically through language (written and verbal) and numbers.

Since 2000, Bruner has been involved in a project called SUMIT (Schools with Success). The factors associated with success appear to include collaboration amongst staff, a focus on the arts across the curriculum, and assessment embedded in meaningful activities. His twenty first century activities have included an increasing emphasis on the role of culture in schooling and on the role of story in shaping learning and understanding.

What does practice look like?

Bruner's idea of a LASS (see glossary) can be seen in many interactions between adults and babies – as the caregiver tries to find ways to draw the baby into language and communication. Peek-a-boo games are a good example of this since they introduce the baby to the turn-taking necessary for good communication.

A spiral curriculum can also be seen in everyday practice. This is linked to the notion of constructing knowledge and of building on existing knowledge. Educationalists know that children learn best if we begin from prior knowledge and from interests. A spiral curriculum enables children to return and develop learning over time. Rather than pressing on with too much knowledge in a particular area, the wise practitioner comes back to particular ideas and concepts over a period of time.

The emphasis on a wide range of materials with which children may represent ideas, events or feelings is firmly linked to Bruner's idea of stages. At first, children represent things with their bodies – thinking begins with the physical – an idea that is borne out by increased understanding of the importance of physical development. As experience increases, children (or indeed adult learners) begin to visualise or develop mental images. Gradually, these mental images (or icons) give way to symbols which may not seem to be like the thing they stand for. In order to allow children to develop towards abstract or symbolic thinking, practitioners encourage choice and provide opportunities to translate their ideas from one type of media to another. As in Reggio Emilia, practitioners emphasise the Hundred Languages of Children, so encouraging children to sing about, draw about, make models and act out their ideas or experiences helps them to move toward symbolic thought.

His influence

Howard Gardner[1] has described Jerome Bruner as having no peers when it comes to enlarging our sense of how children learn and what educators could aspire to. He has developed the skills of many leading educationalists and developmental psychologists. Professor Kathy Sylva, from the Institute of Education, University of London, has worked with him. She is known for her involvement with the Effective Provision of Pre-school Education (EPPE) Project. So have Howard Gardner (see page 87) and Margaret Donaldson (see page 83). Gardner describes Bruner as a 'communicator, model and identification figure'.

Bruner's work on stage development has been widely taken up because it matches practitioners' perceptions of how learning and thought actually occur. Similarly, the notion of a spiral curriculum is popular since it chimes with current ideas about how the brain develops – concepts are gradually modified as experience increases. Overall, Bruner has successfully influenced thinking and practice in many fundamental ways.

Common criticisms of his theory

Bruner criticised his programme *Man: a course of study* as being too elitist or intellectual and too much concerned with non-American issues. He claimed that it worked best with well prepared teachers working with advantaged pupils and that it had an excessive focus on the learner as an individual rather than as a member of a culture or society. The Oxford Pre-School Research was criticised by early childhood practitioners in Britain when it was published in the 1980s. This may be because Bruner appeared to not entirely understand what practitioners were aiming to do. Despite this, thirty or more years on, his comments on early childhood education still ring true. He argues that we know how to improve young children's life chances, and that although the economy is stretched the benefits of offering nursery education "would not be costly. The return in kindling human hope for the future would be great"[5].

GLOSSARY

Scaffolding: process by which an adult or more experienced learner helps a child to take small supported steps towards his or her intended goal.

Spiral curriculum: a curriculum that revisits ideas repeatedly, building upon earlier learning each time they are met again.

Enactive representation: understanding is developed in action as children handle objects, play and move.

Iconic representation: children begin to create mental images and may not need physical reminders.

Symbolic representation: abstract ideas, including language use, can be used to represent the world around.

LASS: language acquisition support system or, more simply, a mother.

POINTS FOR REFLECTION

○ Collect some examples of children representing experiences or ideas physically or through a variety of media, such as blocks, paint, dressing up etc. Are these enactive, iconic or symbolic in your view?

○ Ask one of your colleagues to observe you when you are attempting to scaffold a child's learning. Discuss how effective you think you were.

○ Why have we not been more successful in helping policy makers to value high quality early education more? How can we do better?

Chris Athey and schema theory

PROFILE

Chris Athey changed the way in which the cognitive development of children between the ages of 2 and 5 is understood. Her writing, together with other notables including Tina Bruce and Cathy Nutbrown, continues to influence practice.

KEY DATES

1924	Born in South Shields
1973-1978	Froebel Early Education Project
1990	*Extending Thought in Young Children* is published
2011	Dies, following a series of operations

LINKS

Piaget
Bruner

Trajectory schema?

Her life

Christine Athey was born in South Shields in north-east England, in 1924. She left school at 13, taking up a variety of odd jobs. When war broke out, she moved to Croydon and attended a series of workers' education classes extending both her general education and her knowledge of psychology. At the end of the war, Athey trained as a teacher and taught in east London where she met many challenges – lack of resources; and classes of up to 60 children, many of whom had faced serious trauma and deprivation during the war years. Even at this early stage in her career she had a firm belief in the importance of working with the parents of young children.

Athey began to teach at Ibstock Place, the school linked to the Froebel Educational Institute (now part of Roehampton University). While there, she studied for the Froebel training diploma, and subsequently completed a master's degree. In 1973, she was appointed as director of The Froebel Educational Institute Project the results of which were to have a significant impact on early childhood education. Tina Bruce (now emeritus professor in early childhood studies at the University of Roehampton, based at Froebel College) worked as her research assistant. Athey continued as principal lecturer for many years at the Froebel Institute.

Chris Athey continued to be active and vociferous in the field of early childhood in her latter years. She worked with staff at the Pen Green Children's Centre and Research Base as a pedagogue, guiding practice there. After a period of ill health and a series of operations, Chris Athey died in 2011.

Her writing

Chris Athey was not a prolific writer but she was meticulous.

Athey's research involved stimulating trips for the experimental group

Although the Froebel research project finished in 1978, the book outlining her findings was not published until 1990. A second edition of the book was produced seventeen years after that.

- 'Humour in Children related to Piaget's theory of intellectual development' in Chapman, A. and Foot, H. (eds) *It's a Funny Thing, Humour* (Pergamon Press, 1977)

- 'Parental Involvement in nursery education' *Early Childhood Development and Care* 7:4 (1981)

- *Extending Thought in Young Children* (Paul Chapman Publishing, 1990) (2nd ed, 2007)

Her theory

In 1973 Athey set up the Froebel Early Education Project which lasted for five years, researching aspects of young children's development. A group of about 20 children that she described as 'disadvantaged'

were observed for two years. Over the same period, a control group of socio-economically advantaged children was also studied.

The project had three main aims[1]:

- To produce information on the ways in which knowledge is acquired by young children at home and school.

- To provide an effective enrichment programme for children from a disadvantaged section of the community.

- To document a number of developmental sequences of behaviour from early motor behaviours to 'thought', in sufficient detail to allow professionals to evaluate the data and the usefulness of interpretation.

Children attending the research nursery were taken on regular visits, generally with their parents, to places of interest. Their subsequent play was carefully observed and analysed. The children's representation of what they had experienced might be seen in play, drawings, block play, language or movements.

The data collected led Athey to use the term 'schema' to describe children's activity. The term is widely used in psychology and associated in particular with Piaget. Chris Athey applied the theory to the practical observation and analysis of young children's learning. For Chris Athey[1] there are many different definitions of schema but no single one on which everyone would agree. She suggests that in Piaget's early work he used schema to mean the general cognitive structures which are developing in children under the age of five. Athey explains how children use schema to arrive at categories and classifications. For example, a baby learns by banging a wide range of objects, and by trying out a wide range of schema on a single object, whether or not the object is bangable, suckable, throwable, shakable and so on. This underlines the importance of rich and varied experience.

Over time, Athey suggested, schema can be put together to create higher level and more powerful schemas. Schema theory can be used, for example, to explain the results obtained by Piaget in his conservation tests (see page 48). When a child is unable to say that two rows of counters are the same even though they know that there are ten in each row, Donaldson's (see page 84) explanation is that the context does not make 'human sense' to the child. Schema theory can be interpreted as suggesting that although the child has a number or quantity schema as well as a length schema they are not yet able to consider both at the same time. The dominant or more important of the two schema for young children is likely to be length and this is the concept which dominates their response to the question.

According to Athey[1], schema evolve from early action and perception. They are part of the way in which children seek to make sense of their environment and relationships. The analysis of observations, drawings and paintings led the project team to identify a number of schemas. Children are described as having four stages in exploring and using schema:

1. A period of physical action where the movement does not carry any real significance.
2. A stage when schema are used to symbolise something.
3. Children may begin to see the functional relationship between two things.
4. The schema supports thought.

Putting the theory into practice

An example of these stages might be a child interested in rotation. At the first stage they might simply spend time twirling around. Over time, the twirling might be used to describe or symbolise a merry-go-round. The child may become interested in the relationship between a reel of fishing line and the way in which it acts to change the length of line – shortening and lengthening it depending on the direction in which it is turned. Finally, the child becomes able to put all these ideas into words and to reason and think about them. Numerous schema were identified in the research project. These included:

- Vertical;

- Back and forth or side to side;

- Circular or rotational;

- Going over, under or on top of;

- Going round a boundary;

- Containing and enveloping;

- Going through a boundary.

Tina Bruce[2] describes the importance and usefulness of schema for identifying the consistent thread of interest that a child may have. She suggests that this can be hidden from the educator if he or she concentrates simply on the content of the child's interest. She quotes Chris Athey as saying that 'frequently ... children shift from one kind of content to another within the same period. When they do this they are

---

What does practice look like?

Fundamental to the application of schema theory to practice is that practitioners need to observe children in free play, identify and extend their dominant schema. This one aspect alone has helped to change perceptions about the value of children's play. The apparent randomness of children's actions can, in the light of schema theory, be seen as a series of connected activities. For example, an interest in dinosaurs' teeth, stairs, birds' wings and the letters M and W may reveal an interest in zigzags. Practitioners can extend children's interest by offering pinking shears, zigzag combs for painting or materials which can be laid out in a zigzag pattern. Similarly, an interest in the story of Rapunzel may be linked to a preferred vertical schema. Practitioners could extend this by providing blocks for building high; or pulleys and ropes for lifting objects high and letting them down again.

In baby and toddler rooms, for example, there will be a stage at which most, if not all children, will want to hide their faces and delight in an adult saying 'boo' when the scarf is removed. Similarly, young children delight in stuffing bags and boxes full of random items. The provision of scarves or small pieces of fabric and a collection of bags of various shapes and sizes will cater for the needs of children engaging in a 'going over' or 'covering' schema or a 'containing' schema respectively.

One important benefit of the approach is in work with parents. Where parents are introduced to the theory it helps them to understand children's interests and activity as helpful to development rather than simply a nuisance. It can also help them (as well as practitioners) to find ways to channel the interest or schema into more acceptable behaviour. So, for example, a child enjoying a trajectory schema is likely to take great delight in throwing things. He or she can be given bean bags and a basket to make up a scoring game or sort laundry into different boxes for each member of the family.

accused of flitting ... and so they might be... but they are also fitting. They are fitting various kinds of content into a particular schema'.

The point about schema theory is that it is happening in practice all the time. Whatever their dominant interest of the moment children will find ways to move or represent their ideas in ways which include their preferred schema. For members of staff who plan to meet children's schema, the provision must support children in a variety of ways. Children who are interested in trajectories, for example, need materials that will enable them to throw things safely and in new challenging ways.

Her influence

Athey's work has been highly influential. In addition to her own account of work on schema, Professor Tina Bruce (who worked on the project) has published widely on the subject and is internationally renowned. Cathy Nutbrown has also written about schema. John Matthews has published work on the role of schema in developing mark-making and Cath Arnold (of the Pen Green Children's Centre) has more recently written about schema and attachment. Pen Green itself has worked with both Tina Bruce and Chris Athey as pedagogues in developing their understanding of the theory and its application.

Schema-spotting has become an important pedagogical and analytical tool in many early years settings. It is particularly useful with very young children whose actions can appear random. Once practitioners begin to scrutinise their observations they begin to see patterns of behaviour which can be addressed through rich and varied provision. It helps practitioners too to identify resources which are likely to be used by most children at particular ages and stages.

It can also be helpful in supporting parents' understanding of their children's learning and development.

Common criticisms of her theory

No work has been done on identifying the developmental aspects of schemas. It is unclear whether children get stuck on a particular preferred schema or whether they move from schema to schema. The frequency with which particular schemas were found in the movements and representations of children at different ages in the project suggests that there may be a developmental scale of schemas. This has not yet been worked on. There is a danger that 'schema-spotting' could trivialise observations of children's learning. Simply spotting the schema may not lead to extension and support.

Julian Grenier[3] argues that the theory has not been rigorously evaluated. Both Athey and her followers have accepted the basis of her theory, which is Piagetian – at a time when much of Piaget's thinking about cognitive development has been questioned. In particular, while Piaget sees the sensori-motor stage as focusing on children under two years of age, Athey's study included only children of three and over. Grenier suggests[4] that schema theory may be of most value in working with up to threes rather than older children.

Enveloping or containing?

POINTS FOR REFLECTION

○ Do you think schema theory is of equal value when working with babies and toddlers as when working with older children?

○ What schematic interests can you identify in the children you are working with?

○ How can parents be introduced to schema theory? Would it be helpful to them?

Loris Malaguzzi and early education in Reggio Emilia

PROFILE

Loris Malaguzzi was the teacher who developed the philosophy and who became the founding director of the world's most famous nursery schools. His commitment to children and community has developed over more than sixty years.

KEY DATES

1920	Born
1945	The first nurseries open in Reggio Emilia
1963	Appointed head of Reggio Emilia's first municipal nursery
1970	The first municipal centres for birth to three-year-olds open
1994	Dies

LINKS

Dewey
Piaget
Vygotsky
Gardner
Bruner
Erikson
Montessori
Froebel

His life

In 1945, after the Second World War, a group of parents in Reggio Emilia, Northern Italy, decided that they wanted to build their own school. Loris Malaguzzi, a teacher, said that the nursery was 'created and run by parents...in a devastated town, rich only in mourning and poverty', funded from 'the sale of an abandoned war tank, a few trucks, and some horses left behind by the retreating Germans'.[1]

Careful observation is encouraged

Malaguzzi was so inspired by the courage and motivation of these parents that he changed his job so that he could teach in the first centre, Villa Cella. Through his leadership and inspiration more parent-run centres grew. In 1963, city funding was provided for a new centre and by 1967 parental pressure had led to all the parent-run schools coming under the administration of the municipality of Reggio Emilia.

Around the time of his death in 1994, a non-profit making organisation was formed, namely the Friends of Reggio Children International Association. Its aim was to promote the work of Malaguzzi through professional development. In 2006 the Loris Malaguzzi International Centre opened with the grandiose aim of improving the lives of people and communities, in Reggio Emilia and beyond, through education and research.

The centres are characterised by the attention they give to involving everyone in learning. Parents, children, professional staff and the wider community are all seen as part of the education process. Reggio Emilia educators value all aspects of children's development. Children are viewed in terms of their strengths, not weaknesses, and are given credit for their capacity to learn. The results are seen in the aesthetic environments of the schools, the spirit of co-operation between staff, parents and children and in the quality of children's representational work.

His writing

Malaguzzi may have been engaged in writing numerous policy documents but there is very little available in his own words.

The seminal work on Reggio Emilia is *The Hundred Languages of Children* and in the first edition published in 1995 included an interview with him, recorded by Gandini. That is no longer included in the more recent third edition.

A small book entitled *A journey into the rights of children* is credited to Malaguzzi and his colleagues but was published in 1995, after his death. It mainly consists of children's thoughts, discussions and interpretations of their rights. The words are those of children aged five and six.

Malaguzzi comments[2] that "what made the greatest impression on us was the children's sense of justice and equality, the social maturity of their judgement, a real feeling of responsibility and solidarity".

His theory

Malaguzzi based the philosophy which he brought to the nurseries of Reggio Emilia on the work of Dewey, Piaget, Vygotsky and Erikson. Gardner adds to this list of influences, Froebel and Montessori. Over time, a theoretical underpinning has evolved which give the schools a distinctive style and approach. The key principles include[3]:

1. All children have potential;
2. Children are connected (to their family community, society, objects, symbols);
3. The reciprocity of children (meaning that they not only want to receive but to give);
4. Children are communicators;
5. The environment is the third teacher;
6. Educators are partners, nurturers and guides;

Painting is one of the hundred languages of children

7. Educators are researchers;
8. Documentation as a learning tool;
9. Families as partners.

Putting the theory into practice

The small town of Reggio Emilia now has 78 municipal preschools and infant toddler centres all of which subscribe to a belief that children are, and must be treated as, strong, powerful and competent. Creativity, listening to children, community involvement, and, in line with Dewey's vision, democratic citizenship are key to their work.

The centres are characterised by the attention they give to involving everyone in learning. Parents, children, professional staff and the wider community are all seen as part of the education process. Reggio Emilia educators value all aspects of children's development. Children are viewed in terms of their strengths, not weaknesses, and are given credit for their capacity to learn. The results are seen in the aesthetic environments of the schools, the spirit of co-operation between staff, parents and children, and in the quality of children's representational work.

The curriculum in the Reggio Emilia pre-school centres is built around a range of visual and expressive arts. Children are given opportunities to represent their experiences, ideas, thoughts and feelings in a variety of 'languages'. Thinking and learning are believed to be promoted by the 'translation' from one language to another. So, a child may observe and draw the lions in the town square but will also be encouraged to move like a lion, paint and model lions, act out a shadow play about lions, and talk about lions.

A pedagogista (or curriculum coordinator) works with a number of settings and helps the team to identify a progettazione (or learning context). Observation of children is continuous and provides an understanding of learning way beyond an individual child but on wider development. From their observations, staff produce pedagogical documentation which is used in an attempt to review and analyse what happens during group experiences without predetermined expectations.

The group activities or experiences are based on clear principles[4]:

- learning groups contain adults as well as children;

- documenting learning helps to make learning visible and thus open to further development;

- members of learning groups are engaged in the emotional and aesthetic, as well as the intellectual dimensions of learning;

- the focus of learning in learning groups goes beyond the individual and creates a collective body of knowledge.

Children are encouraged to translate ideas from one medium to another

What does practice look like?

Every nursery has an atelierista whose job is to promote children's visual, aesthetic and creative representations. After discussion with the pedagogista, the atelierista makes sure that the workshops (or ateliers), which are an integral part of provision in all the nurseries, are maintained to high standards and equipped with stimulating materials.

An emphasis on reflection is symbolised by the widespread use of light, glass and mirrors. Spotlights, overhead projectors and shadow screens, are used to create images on screens and walls. Mirror lined boxes encourage children to look at reflections. Mirrors are placed so that children can observe themselves and others, monitoring and rehearsing facial expressions.

Record-keeping is the ultimate responsibility of the atelierista who makes sure that documentation is kept. Children's responses to activities and experiences are recorded in photographs, videos, written observations, transcripts of children's comments and conversations, and of course children's drawings, models, paintings and other creative endeavours. Documentation is analysed and reviewed by staff in their continuous efforts to observe, identify and understand children's learning. In their view, formal assessment is only necessary if you do not believe that learning is visible.

Reggio Children's website contains many fine examples of the kinds of projects or progettaziones that are undertaken. They produce books and DVDs illustrating the children's work that has been undertaken in these world-renowned settings.

Children are connected

Common criticisms of his theory

Loris Malaguzzi's approach grew up in a particular context for a particular community. It cannot be moved from one culture to another. A former mayor of the town said[3] that, having been subjected to a Fascist regime, the citizens had decided that 'people who conformed and obeyed were dangerous' and that it was therefore imperative 'to communicate that lesson and nurture a vision of children who can think and act for themselves'.

Peter Moss, Professor of Early Childhood Provision at London Institute of Education and a researcher at Thomas Coram Research Centre, says that 'Reggio does not offer a recipe nor a method and cannot be copied because (the) values (on which it is based) can only be lived'.[5]

There are also concerns to do with race, gender and class. One Reggio parent comments that 'until recently the cultural mix wasn't an issue. It was a very wealthy area..... Now there are immigrants .... who bring problems.... The people of Reggio do not want to change'.[6] Given that this is a society that has not had to deal with the challenge of cultural diversity, and where gender issues have not been high on the agenda, some writers question the extent to which practitioners in this country should seek to imitate the work of Reggio Emilia.

His influence

As the fame of the schools spread, Jerome Bruner (see pages 63-66), Lilian Katz (an internationally known American professor of early childhood education), and Howard Gardner (see pages 87-91) became interested in and excited by the work in Reggio Emilia. Howard Gardner has developed a close link with the schools, working to compare both the theory and the practice which surrounds Project Zero at Harvard University (see page 90) and the work of Reggio children. Those who visit Reggio Emilia are impressed by the quality of the work which children produce, by the beauty of the environments created with children and by the sense of community support and involvement.

There are attempts to emulate the work of Reggio Emilia around the world, particularly in the United States and New Zealand where early years teachers receive some training in the approach. In Sweden, there is a Reggio Emilia Institute. What should not be forgotten is the longevity of the provision. While Dewey ran his school for four years and wrote about it for decades after, Reggio Emilia's nurseries – the brainchild of Loris Malaguzzi have been open for more than sixty years and continue to flourish.

Lessons to be learnt from Reggio Emilia are the emphases on respect for the children and their families; and on taking time to genuinely see and hear what children say and do. Simply looking and listening is not enough. Reggio practitioners remind us all that this is vital to effective practice and involve openness, patience, concentration and genuine interest. They are not alone in their belief but they are forthright in acting as advocates for this respectful approach.

GLOSSARY

Atelier: workshop or studio with a vast range of creative media.

Atelierista: teacher trained in art education and team leader in respect of curriculum and documentation.

Pedagogista: teaching coordinator working as a consultant in a number of schools and centres.

Progettazione: learning contexts or projects.

POINTS FOR REFLECTION

○ What can you do to improve your ability to really see and hear children?

○ Do you offer children encouragement to transform or translate their ideas from one medium into another? What steps can you take to improve their opportunities?

○ Review the nine key principles of Malaguzzi's theory listed above. Are there any that you would like to develop further in your setting?

Paulo Freire

PROFILE

Paulo Freire was a Brazilian social activist, educator and education theorist. During his exile he worked in many parts of the world to transform the life chances of disadvantaged groups. Once he was able to return to Brazil he set about improving the education of adults and children.

KEY DATES

1921	Born
1964	Exiled to Chile
1979	Returns to Brazil
1997	Dies

LINKS

Fromm
Dewey

Love of life is valued

His life

Paulo Freire was born in 1921 in Recife, Brazil. Freire worked with peasant workers, mainly in the impoverished areas of north-eastern Brazil, developing ways of dealing with the problems of widespread illiteracy. Following his exile to Chile, he became engaged in educational programmes in various countries including Chile, Angola, Mozambique, Cape Verde, Guinea-Bissau and Nicaragua. He worked as a consultant for UNESCO.

Political changes in Brazil meant that Freire could return there in 1979 and following elections won by the Workers' Party he became Secretary of Education. He launched several progressive programmes including those dealing with adult education, curricular restructuring, community participation and policies for democratising schools. For Freire, education was political. He emphasised the importance of praxis, which he defined as action linked to reflection.

Freire did not want his ideas to become accepted without question as he believed that education is inextricably linked to culture. Freire's theories drew on Eric Fromm's ideas from whom he quotes as follows[1]:

Freedom to create and to construct, to wonder and to venture, such freedom requires that the individual be active and responsible, not a slave or a well-fed cog in the machine... It is not enough that men are slaves; if social conditions further the existence of automatons, the result will not be love of life, but love of death.

His writing

Freire wrote a number of books but few have been translated into English. His most influential book world-wide has been *Pedagogy of the Oppressed* (Penguin, 1972).

His theory

Freire's work[2] was about transformation. It sought to change existing practices, rules, traditions and understandings as a way of achieving social justice and equality. He used social activism and social reconstructionism – drawing inspiration from liberation struggles in different parts of Latin America. For Freire, education should seek to make the individual a morally, intellectually and politically engaged activist so that society and its values can be transformed and so extend the possibility of justice to all. Change theorists, such as Freire,

Literacy is seen as key to democracy

wanted children to be able to critically analyse their daily lives. The transformation he sought was about:

- transforming individuals into people who would be politically, intellectually and morally engaged in society; and

- transforming society to create more justice and fairness in public life.

Putting the theory into practice

Freire was concerned with changing ideas. His aim was to promote equality of opportunity by helping children to deal with the fair and unfair. He wanted them to work in an environment where they cooperated in creating a living democracy and building social action skills. The classroom for Freire, therefore, involved learners talking and exploring ideas, learning with the teacher rather than from them. It should enable learners to embrace freedom and to change their world. He challenged existing approaches to education believing that it:

- had been shaped by history;

- involved social consequences;

- was political and thus unfairly shaped the lives of poor or oppressed people;

- was inherently problematic.

His influence

Freire worked in disadvantaged communities to increase their involvement in democracy and education. In some of those places, transformational theories have had a vital role to play in tackling inequalities and he has promoted an awareness of the power needed to transform society.

His work has influenced writers such as Giroux. It has also been suggested that the term 'hidden curriculum' arose from Freire's work. Praxis is a term frequently used in leadership and management writings.

What does practice look like?

Fundamental to Freire's approach is the notion that it should enlighten the masses. Injustice comes in many forms and approaches to education which, like Freire, seek to change the status quo, are also varied. Those prioritising gender injustice may seek to ensure that:

- children's play is not stereotyped;

- boys and girls engage in challenging physical play and take on caring roles;

- practitioners make use of songs, rhymes and stories that challenge gender stereotypes.

Practitioners highlighting anti-racist and multiculturalism may focus on:

- celebration of cultural diversity;

- challenging the impact of bias on individuals and groups.

Overall, those adopting a change agenda need to adopt a reflective approach so that they do not become blind to injustices[2]. This may involve:

- building children's self-esteem and pride;

- helping children to be comfortable with diversity;

- recognising and challenging unfairness.

Common criticisms of his theory

Social reconstruction requires co-operation and a genuine desire for change. For Freire, the greatest danger would be for his ideas to become tokens or slogans. He is sometimes criticised for being too mystical. His rhetoric can be seen as simplistic, rooted in black and white. He has also been criticised as having an outmoded view of literacy and the way in which reading and writing are best acquired.

GLOSSARY

Praxis: action linked to reflection.

POINTS FOR REFLECTION

○ What steps do you take to ensure an anti-bias curriculum?

○ How can practitioners help children to feel unfairness?

○ How can children be given a greater voice in what happens in the setting?

Freire championed the poor and oppressed

David Weikart and the HighScope approach

PROFILE

HighScope is an approach that was developed by Dr David Weikart to serve children at risk of school failure in Ypsilanti, Michigan, USA. The name signifies 'high aspirations and breadth of vision'. The curriculum model is now used in more than 20 countries including UK, Ireland, Mexico, the Netherlands, Indonesia, Korea and South Africa.

KEY DATES

1931	Weikart born in Ohio
1962	HighScope Perry Pre-school Project in Ypsilanti, Michigan, USA, began with the first group of 123 children
1984	Publication of *Changed Lives: The Effects of the Perry Preschool Program on Youth through Age 19* by J. R. Berrueta-Clement (HighScope Press)
1990	HighScope UK, the first Institute outside of the US, was formed
2003	Weikart dies of leukaemia
2004	Publication of *Lifetime Effects: The HighScope Perry Pre-school Study through Age 40* by L. Schweinhart (HighScope Press)

LINKS

Piaget
Vygotsky
Erikson
Dewey

His life

Weikart was born in Ohio in 1931, one of four children. His parents were social workers and teachers. Their commitment to helping others was to influence his choices. After graduating in psychology, Weikart was enlisted in 1953 and served in Korea and Japan.

In 1956, he enrolled for a PhD in education and psychology at the University of Michigan. While studying, he took part-time work as a school psychologist for the Ypsilanti Public Schools. Concerned about the underperformance of students in Ypsilanti's poorest neighbourhoods, Weikart worked with some colleagues to devise the Perry Preschool Project. They focused on creating a program for three- and four-year-olds to help them succeed in the school system.

His writing

David Weikart's writing is mainly in the form of reports on the longitudinal study. Much is now out of print. *Educating Young Children: Active Learning Practices for Preschool and Child Care Programs* (2nd Edition, 2002) co-written with Mary Hohmann formed a very effective guide to practice when HighScope was new to practitioners in this country. The HighScope Foundation (www.highscope.org) offers a range of publications.

His theory

Perry Preschool's program focused on each child's intellectual maturation and based on a philosophy of active learning. The HighScope approach is influenced by the writing of Jean Piaget. Piaget's theory of development supported the original curriculum team's philosophical orientation toward active learning. Through active learning – having direct and immediate experiences and deriving meaning from them through reflection – young children make sense of their world. The power of active learning comes from personal initiative.

Children act on their natural desire to explore – they ask and search for answers to questions about people, materials, events and ideas that arouse their curiosity; they solve problems that stand in the way of their goals, and they generate strategies to overcome barriers.

As the approach developed, the teachers involved in the project concentrated on the pragmatics of integrating theory and daily classroom practice, but stuck to the central principles. These are illustrated in the wheel of learning (see facing page). The sections that surround the hub support the child to be an active learner and should be viewed as playing an equal role.

Small group time with a key person

ASSESSMENT
- Teamwork
- Daily anecdotal notes
- Daily planning
- Child assessment

ADULT-CHILD INTERACTION
- Interaction strategies
- Encouragement
- Problem-solving approach to conflict

ACTIVE LEARNING
Initiative
Key experiences

DAILY ROUTINE
- Plan-Do-Review
- Small-group time
- Large-group time

LEARNING ENVIRONMENT
- Areas
- Materials
- Storage

From 1962 to 1967, the HighScope Perry Preschool Project (as it became) was evaluated in a randomised controlled trial of 123 low-income children. It was one of a number of Head Start programmes set up in the USA in the 1960s but it was unique in committing to a longitudinal study designed to examine the long-term effectiveness of the HighScope Curriculum.

A group of children aged three were chosen and assigned to either an intervention group or a non-intervention group. The intervention group attended a high quality early years setting for two and a half hours a day for two years. The teachers also visited the children at home to work with their parents and explain the approach.

At various intervals throughout the past 40 years researchers have gathered information on both groups from age three through to 11, and again at 14, 15, 19, 27 and 40 years old. The results have consistently shown positive outcomes, both educational and social, for the group receiving early intervention. Early results found that the programme group was less likely to need remedial support, and more likely to show greater persistence, independence, problem-solving ability and motivation.

At age 40, the findings showed:

- significantly more of those who had been to a HighScope preschool were employed than were those who had not (76% v 62%);

- the programme group had higher earnings at both 27 and 40;

- the programme group were involved in fewer crimes;

- there was less reliance on welfare benefit and more likelihood of home ownership;

- more programme than no programme males raised their own children (57% v 30%).

Putting the theory into practice

The HighScope approach is based on 40 years of research and practice. Staff encourage children to become decision-makers and problem-solvers, helping them to develop skills and traits that enable them to become successful students as they grow older. HighScope also encourages managers to value training and encourages parents, caregivers and teachers to extend their expectations for children and themselves.

The pre-school curriculum is based on three basic criteria:

- A coherent theory about teaching and learning must guide the curriculum development process;

Group routines are established

- Curriculum theory and practice must support each child's capacity to develop individual talents and abilities through ongoing opportunities for active learning;

- The teachers, researchers and administrators must work as partners in all aspects of the curriculum development, to ensure that theory and practice receive equal consideration.

Staff regularly make anecdotal observations on the children's learning experiences and this forms the basis for planning and evaluating. Learning occurs in a way which meets the needs of the children and is based on their interests and prior learning. The curriculum is framed by a series of developmentally appropriate indicators (for children up to three) and key developmental indicators (for children from 3 to 6 years of age). The indicators are regularly reviewed in the light of current research and ideas of best practice. Key developmental indicators include:

- Approaches to learning;

- Language, literacy and communication;

- Social and emotional development;

- Physical development, health and well-being;

- Mathematics (seriation, number, space);

- Science and technology (classification, time);

- Social studies (participating on group routines; being sensitive to the feelings, needs and interests of others);

- The arts (visual art, dramatic art, music).

His influence

Studies, conducted over many years, show many benefits gained by attending a HighScope preschool for individuals, families and society. HighScope has also had an impact in the classroom. Positioning materials so that they are readily available to children, providing clear visual information that enables children to put resources away so that another child can easily find them and scheduling group times and opportunities for self-initiated learning are not unique to HighScope. They have, however, been presented in systematic ways that enable practitioners to create coherent learning environments.

HighScope practice has been praised[1] for allowing 'children to...see the relationships between objects and events' and for asking questions that promote problem-solving, listening and evaluation. Encouraging children to evaluate, reflect on or review what they have done is very helpful in the learning process.' The HighScope Educational Foundation has been active in exploring the needs of babies and toddlers, as well as the older children that form part of the longitudinal study and in expanding the knowledge that we have of children's development.

What does practice look like?

HighScope practice includes key elements:

- **Positive adult-child interaction** – active learning depends on positive adult-child interaction. Guided by an understanding of how pre-school children think and reason, adults practise positive interaction strategies, sharing control with children, focusing on children's strengths, forming authentic relationships with children, supporting play, adopting a problem solving approach to social conflict and using encouragement, rather than a system based on praise, punishment and reward. This enables children to express thoughts and feelings and confidently decide on the direction and content of the conversation, and experience partnership in dialogue.

- **Well-organised learning environment** – the HighScope approach places a strong emphasis on the layout of the pre-school and providing appropriate materials to enable children to make choices and decisions.

- **The daily routine** – adults plan a consistent routine that supports active learning. This routine enables young children to anticipate what will happen next and gives them a great deal of control over what they do during each part of their day. HighScope provides for a balance of child and teacher initiation. The part of the daily routine which is initiated by the adult is small group time, which usually occurs after the plan-do-review cycle.

- **The plan-do-review process** – during the plan-do-review process children learn to create and express intentions. In a group or individually, and supported by an adult, children plan what they want to do. Their planning becomes more sophisticated as they become used to the process. The youngest child may point, an older child may draw or write their plan. Children then go on to create experiences based upon their plans. They need time for trial and error, generating new ideas, practising and succeeding. Personal independence is the key to active learning by self-motivated children. Time is given for children to act on their intentions at 'work time'. Finally, children reflect on their experiences.

A high quality curriculum must provide opportunities for children to reflect on their experiences with increasing verbal ability and logic. The time set aside for this process is called 'recall' or 'review'. When these three components are experienced by children they develop a strong sense of self-control and self-discipline. This control is power, not over other people or things, but over oneself.

Understanding what is happening in the environment, realising that those around us are genuinely interested in what we say and do, and knowing that our work and effort will often lead to success, is the type of control that promotes personal satisfaction and motivates productivity. The plan is not a straightjacket. It is seen as the beginning of a process of developing a mastery over one's own destiny.

The rest of the daily routine consists of snack time, outside time, circle time and small group time. Small group time is when the teacher plans an activity for a key experience focus. This provides the balance in the daily routine between adult and child initiated activity and all the children take part. The activity will be planned with the active learning ingredients in mind: materials, manipulation, choice, language from the child and support from the adult. Small group time is an excellent time to assess children's emerging skills and abilities.

A typical day

A typical day begins with children arriving at nursery and being greeted individually by each adult. This is the first step in a daily routine which helps children to understand and predict the order of events in their day, developing their concept of time. The session is broken up into a series of sessions. In addition to time allocated to plan-do-review, there is a snack time, and both a small and large group time. Children have the opportunity to start with their own interests and ideas and are asked 'What do you plan to do today?'. They share ideas and projects with their friends and learn to negotiate, collaborate and develop independence.

Once children have planned the area or areas in which they would like to work, they go and follow their plan. They might plan to work in two or three different areas and put the product of their plans or an artefact related to their plans (such as a model, a book or a drawing/painting) in the area where their recall session will be held so that they will be ready to discuss at that time. These will be ready to discuss at recall time. Work time lasts about 45 minutes to one hour when a warning signal for tidy-up time is given by one of the children. Everybody has the responsibility of tidying up the area they have worked in and when they have finished, to go and help someone else. After tidy-up time, it is recall time.

Children ask each other questions about their work such as:

- How did you manage to get that material to stick to the box?

- What is that bit there?

- What do you like about your model?

Arguably, HighScope's greatest influence in the UK has been the setting up of Sure Start. Treasury officials introduced the then Labour government to Weikart's claims that for every dollar spent on high quality early childhood education, seven or more dollars could be saved. The economic benefits convinced the then Labour government of the value of high quality early education.

Common criticisms of his theory

There are difficulties with all approaches. Education has to be a changing process. Understanding of learning and the needs and expectations of society have changed in the past 40 years and it is important that practice develops in the light of this. When an approach is written down, there can be a tension between maintaining the approach and modifying it. If you make changes, at what point does it cease to be HighScope? The same might also of course be said of the Montessori approach.

HighScope has been criticised both for being too structured and for being too free. Epstein et al.[2] argue that these contrasting viewpoints suggest that the extremes reflect political viewpoints and indicate that HighScope strikes a good balance. HighScope has also been criticised[2] as being too difficult or time consuming – a view that Epstein et al. also refute arguing that HighScope is constantly reviewing training procedures and opportunities.

The plan-do-review process could be open to criticism. Being able to articulate what you are planning to do might be a problem for children whom English is a second language (or children with language delay or learning difficulties). Many HighScope practitioners have excellent strategies for helping children to decide, such as having pictures of resources or examples of the resources to be found in different areas. While skilled and experienced practitioners may make good use of the plan-do-review approach, in the hands of practitioners who do not fully understand the underpinning principles the process may be less satisfactory. For example, sometimes the planning may be reduced to choosing a picture to be hung around the neck. A child who had chosen a picture of a pair of scissors was told that as he had planned to do cutting and sticking that is where he should remain for the work period.

HighScope has influenced classroom organisation

POINTS FOR REFLECTION

○ Consider carefully the plan-do-review approach.
What benefits and difficulties might it pose in your setting?

○ HighScope has been highly successful in capturing the imagination of politicians because of its success in highlighting social and economic benefits of high quality early education. What can other settings learn from HighScope?

○ How does the typical day (see page 81) compare to the day in your setting?

Margaret Donaldson and post-Piagetian theories

PROFILE

Margaret Donaldson is best known for her book *Children's Minds*, published in 1978. She has led post-Piagetian thinking in this country. She and her students, many of whom have become respected academics in their own right, have done a great deal to demystify Piagetian theory.

KEY DATES

1926	Born in Paisley, Scotland
1947	Obtains first class honours degree in French and German at the University of Edinburgh
1953	Graduates with distinction from MEd in psychology
1956	Completes PhD on children's thinking
1957	Works with Piaget
1958	Obtains lectureship in the Department of Psychology at Edinburgh
1978	*Children's Minds* is published
1980	Gains professorship
1992	*Human Minds* is published

LINKS

Piaget
Bruner

Children need to explore symbol systems

Her life

Margaret Donaldson is Emeritus Professor of Developmental Psychology at the University of Edinburgh, where she has studied and worked throughout her career. She was born in Paisley in 1926, the eldest of three children.

When Donaldson began her career in developmental psychology, behaviourism was the dominant theory. She spent a term with Piaget in 1957. Martin Hughes[1] writes that 'she came back impressed by his methods and the scale of his theorising, but not convinced he was necessarily right'. She was also influenced by Vygotsky, and by Bruner, with whom she worked at Harvard for a period during the 1960s. In the same decade, Donaldson set up a nursery in the Department of Psychology at the University of Edinburgh. Her observations of three- to five-year-old children there led to the insights that formed the basis of her book, *Children's Minds*.

Her writing

Donaldson's first book continues to be highly influential thirty five years after it was first published. It has been described by Bruner as 'one of the most powerful, most wisely balanced and best informed books on the development of the child's mind to have appeared...its implications for education are enormous'.

- *Children's Minds* (Fontana, 1978)

- *Early Childhood Development and Education: Readings in Psychology* with R. Grieve and C. Pratt (Blackwell, 1983)

- *Human Minds* (Penguin, 1992)

Her theory

Donaldson came to the conclusion that children's errors or misunderstandings came about because they were not simply responding to what they were being asked to do, but were also seeking to understand the meaning of the task or request. They were seeking to make 'human sense' of the situation. The notion of embedded and disembedded thinking is central to Donaldson's theory. Thinking which is embedded or situated in a familiar context makes human sense, and so is more easily understood by children and open to reason. When children are asked to think outside the limits of human sense, in unfamiliar, unrealistic or abstract contexts, their thinking is disembedded and fails to make sense to them.

Donaldson has applied these ideas to Piaget's work. She shows how young children's apparent limitations, which Piaget attributed to their stage of development, are often a result of the task failing to make human sense to them. In *Children's Minds*, Donaldson describes her own experimental work and that of her students. She first tries to build on and modify Piaget's theory of egocentrism. The three mountains test, which Piaget devised to explore young children's ability to take another point of view (see page 48), does

not allow children to demonstrate their understanding, according to Donaldson. She says that Piaget's task is disembedded and so presents particular difficulties. When Martin Hughes wished to explore children's ability to take another's point of view he devised an embedded test in which a policeman and a naughty boy were placed on a board with intersecting walls. Children were asked to place the boy where he could not be seen by the policeman. Because this task was embedded in a context which children could understand, a far higher proportion of them were able to demonstrate an ability to think in a non-egocentric way than in Piaget's experiments.

Secondly, she describes experiments by James McGarrigle which set out to refine some of Piaget's conservation tasks. In one of the classic Piagetian tasks children are shown two rows of ten counters, and asked whether the two lines are the same or different. When the children have agreed that they are the same, one line is extended so that it looks longer than the other – even though it has the same number of counters. Young children tend to say that the longer line has more counters – although they often know that each line still contains ten objects. McGarrigle devised some variations on this test which involved

Play mirrors experience

a teddy bear. This gave a context for the questions and children were far more likely to respond correctly.

Donaldson argues in *Children's Minds* that 'The better you are at tackling problems without having to be sustained by human sense, the more likely you are to succeed in our education system'.[2] Her theories are often focused on educational failure. This is reflected in her view that 'the hope then is that reading can be taught in such a way as greatly to enhance the child's reflective awareness not only of language as a symbolic system, but of the processes of his own mind'.[2]

Unlike Piaget she stresses that feeling and thought are given the same value – one is not more important than the other. Unlike Piaget, earlier modes do not disappear but form a foundation for later modes of thinking of and feeling (see table below).

Donaldson's view of stage development giving equal value to thinking and feeling

Mode of thinking	Indicative age/may be apparent from:	Description
Point mode	2-3 months the here and now	Thinking is concerned with the here and now.
Line mode	8-9 months specific events	Thinking includes specific events recalled from the past. As children develop, thinking also becomes concerned with the future.
Construct mode	3-4 years	Thinking involves considering how things are in the world or the general nature of things There are two forms: the intellectual construct mode (such as doing sums); and the value-sensing construct mode (such as appreciating a painting or a piece of music).
Transcendent	not achieved by all	Thinking moves beyond mode time and space. There are two forms: the intellectual transcendent mode (such as logic); and the value-sensing transcendent mode (such as spiritual or religious thought).

Putting the theory into practice

Margaret Donaldson's work led many practitioners (and researchers) to reassess the idea of readiness to learn and psychological testing methods. This, in turn, has meant that those working with young children are less ready to accept test findings in which children are required to think in disembedded or formal ways. Piagetian theory led many practitioners, particularly during the 1960s, to think of children having a ceiling on their thinking.

Thinking develops through real-life experience

What does practice look like?

While Piaget showed the intricacies of children's thinking and learning, Donaldson and her students, such as Martin Hughes, demonstrated that ideas must make human sense to children in order to be understood. Over the past thirty years this has been of great importance in shaping the curriculum. Practitioners have understood that familiar starting points – what children already know and understand – are essential to effective learning. They also know that children do not simply respond to what is said to them but that the context, the way in which things are said shaped children's understanding.

Donaldson's insight has now opened further windows on children's thinking. It has encouraged practitioners to consider the child's perspective when presenting new materials. Worthington and Carruthers[3] suggest that in highlighting human sense, Donaldson has made it clear to practitioners that observation must be made from the point of view of 'child sense'. In other words, practice in which practitioners seek to ensure that teaching makes human sense, will be providing opportunities for children to demonstrate what makes sense to them.

This has become commonplace in literacy development where opportunities are provided for children to do their own writing (or have-a-go). This allows adults to see what sense children are making of words and letters. Worthington and Carruthers are attempting to ensure that the same possibility exists with mathematical mark-making. They suggest that adults take time to work out children's current mathematical understanding from their pictures.

Donaldson's challenges to those theories encouraged practitioners to seek out what children are able to do rather than emphasising what they cannot do. This does not mean that Donaldson rejected child-centred education. Indeed, she suggests that the education of young children should be based on a decentred approach. She deliberately chose this Piagetian term because she believed that in order to educate young children effectively, practitioners must 'decentre' and try to present things from the child's viewpoint.

Her influence

In the introduction to *Early Childhood Development and Education,* Donaldson identifies three trends in developmental psychology. She suggests that we are now able to see more clearly the importance of interpersonal relationships in developing language and thought. Secondly, we have begun to understand the special demands that are made on children when we ask them to undertake disembedded tasks. Thirdly, we are much more aware of the importance in attempting to understand children's learning, focusing on what they can do rather than what they cannot do.

Donaldson has challenged the orthodoxy of both teaching and developmental psychology. Moreover she has identified the importance (and some of the limitations) of child-centred education. She is not alone in stressing the equal value of intellect and emotion – but her clear and accessible writing have made this apparent to a wide audience.

Margaret Carr argues that theorists such as Margaret Donaldson have changed understanding of staged development. While Piaget's suggested that the stages led to a state of logical, reasoned mature thought, Donaldson (and others including Bruner) have led to a better understanding of the 'multiple ways of thinking and knowing' in which humans engage. This means that the contributions of earlier stages of development to thinking is valued as and feeling is given greater value 'renewed value to the here and now, originally seen in Piagetian terms as an immature stage of development'[4].

Common criticisms of her theory

Piaget's work has been criticised as having led to approaches with too much focus on the child and too little on what must be learnt. Although Donaldson's theories have both challenged Piaget's work and given greater understanding on the child's point of view, her work has not been sufficiently developed to enable practitioners to make full use of her ideas.

GLOSSARY

Embedded thinking: ideas which are situated (or embedded) in a familiar context or experience make better every day, or human, sense to children.

Disembedded thinking: ideas which are without context (or disembedded) are more difficult for children to understand since they are abstract.

POINTS FOR REFLECTION

- Look for examples of situations where children appear to misunderstand because they are seeking to make human sense of a situation.

- Analyse a child's mark-making. Try to identify the development of the child's understanding of symbols. Is he or she using formal letters or numbers or representing these concepts in some other way?

- Look at video which presents Piaget's three mountain task (e.g. http://www.youtube.com/watch?v=GIXN-JYrNC8 and/ or http://www.youtube.com/watch?v=v4oYOjVDgo0). Try to identify why Donaldson described this as a disembedded task. How could children be helped to understand better what they were asked to do?

Learning should focus on what children can do

How children learn

Howard Gardner and multiple intelligence theory

PROFILE

Howard Gardner has worked in many fields of psychology. A self-styled 'old student of the brain', he developed the multiple intelligence theory. Gardner's work continues to influence current understanding of learning and creativity.

KEY DATES

1943   Born in Pennsylvania, USA

1961   Begins studying at Harvard University, where he has remained throughout his career.

1983   *Frames of Mind* is published, setting out multiple intelligence theory

LINKS

Erikson
Piaget
Bruner
Malaguzzi

Pattern recognition reflects natural intelligence

His life

Howard Gardner is Professor of Cognition and Education at Harvard University but has worked in many areas of psychology. He has been strongly influenced by Bruner (see pages 63-66) with whom he worked early in his career. Gardner is best known for his book, *Frames of Mind*, in which he sets out his multiple intelligence theory (MIT). He admits that he has been influenced by the death of his elder brother, aged only eight, before Howard was even born[1]. He did not know about this tragedy until he discovered a newspaper cutting reporting it. He claims that his motivation for success as a pianist and scholar came from his sense of having to make up in some way for the death of his brother.

In his academic career he was highly influenced by Erik Erikson, one of his tutors at Harvard, and from whom he learned to value careful observation, to regard human personality as the central concern of psychology and to focus on developmental psychology. His early career was unorthodox and the factors that influenced his thinking unusually diverse. Firstly, he won a scholarship and spent a year in London, reading and visiting theatres and galleries. Secondly, he got a job with Bruner who was developing his curriculum project 'Man: a course of study'. Through this project he was introduced to the work of Piaget and Levi-Strauss who studied diverse cultural practices. He took a job for a short time as a teacher of young children and spent some time working with schizophrenic patients.

His writing

Gardner has written many books, dating back to the early 1970s. Many of his books are available in updated versions. As well as *Frames of*

Reflection and interaction are personal intelligences

Mind (Fontana, first published in 1983), titles of particular interest to early childhood practitioners include:

- *The Arts and Human Development* (1973)

- *Artful Scribbles* (1980)

- *The Unschooled Mind: how children think and how schools should teach* (1993)

His theory

Gardner regards intelligence as being 'too important to be left to intelligence testers'.[2] He suggests that 'we must figure out how intelligence and morality can work together to create a world in which a great variety of people will want to live'.

Multiple intelligence theory arose out of Gardner's dissatisfaction with the dominant views of intelligence and learning early in his career. In his book, *Frames of Mind*, Gardner sets out the contributions of major

theorists to our thinking about intelligence. He cites Charles Darwin, the evolutionist, as doing 'more than any other figure to stimulate scientific study of the mind'.[3] He underlines the role of Gesell, who focused on the genetic factors that shape learning. Gesell's research with twins suggested that many aspects of children's maturation were determined by their biology. He set out what Gardner calls 'the orderly milestones of development'[3] by setting up experiments where one twin would be given special training in, for example, climbing stairs while the other was not given any support. In many cases, training made no difference to the twins' ability to perform physical tasks.[3]

Gardner compares this view to that of the behaviourist, Skinner. Skinner believed that 'a human being could learn to do almost anything that his surroundings dictated'.[3] Nurture, or systematic training, could enable rats to run mazes and pigeons to play table tennis. Gardner also discusses the contribution of Piaget, whom he describes as 'beyond question the single dominant thinker in his field'.[3] However, he thought that Piaget placed too little emphasis on the importance of the emotions and of motivation in learning and too much emphasis on logic and number. Gardner also criticises Piaget's notion of staged development with the implications that:

- the stage of development in one area of development is tied to the stage of development in another area;

- as the learner moves from one stage of development to another, they leave behind earlier aspects of development.

Gardner, like Bruner, says that earlier ways of thinking and exploring (such as play) are not left behind as we move towards abstract thinking but can be drawn on to support learning in new areas or experiences. Gardner's work on multiple intelligences arose from his dissatisfaction with the notion of intelligence as something that could be seen or measured and represented as an IQ score. He has set out to explore 'how people are intelligent rather than how much intelligence they have'.[4] He defines intelligence as 'the ability to solve problems or to create products that are valued within one or more cultural settings'.[2] He regards the emergence of intelligences as dependent on the opportunities offered to children within a particular context or culture.

Specific intelligences can be identified, he suggests, because:

- damage to specific areas of the brain causes specific kinds of impairment such as with language;

- savants and prodigies show specific gifts in particular areas such as mathematics and music;

- it is possible to test specific areas, such as spatial awareness, in different ways and to find correlations between these tests;

- a defined developmental process has been identified – again this is the case with language;

- the behaviour can be encoded in a symbol system. Language and mathematics can be written as well as spoken and read.

In the first edition of *Frames of Mind*, published in 1983, Gardner listed seven intelligences which he had identified by using the criteria above. At that stage he suggested that the intelligences were:

- linguistic intelligence;

- musical intelligence;

- logical-mathematical intelligence;

- spatial intelligence;

- bodily-kinaesthetic intelligence;

- interpersonal (interactions with others); and

- intrapersonal (understanding of self) intelligence.

Later, he added naturalist intelligence (concerned with nature, seasons, plant categorisation) and suggested that the two personal intelligences should be seen as permeating all others. He considered and rejected the idea of spiritual intelligence but proposed that we all have an existential intelligence (awareness of something beyond us and our lives) but this intelligence has not been defined in the same detail as others.

A fuller explanation of Gardner's multiple intelligences is below and overleaf.

Linguistic intelligence

Linguistic intelligence is being demonstrated when we use language to:

- convince others

- remember

- explain events, ideas and feelings – this includes story, poetry and metaphors when we say, for example, the sky was a billowing tent

- reflect on language itself, what is called metalinguistic analysis.

Logical-mathematical intelligence

This intelligence:

- is helpful in dealing with some kinds of problems

- in western cultures, this is often given greater status than other intelligences

- should not be seen as more important than others.

Bodily-kinaesthetic intelligence

This intelligence is concerned with all the ways in which humans express ideas in physical ways. Gardner suggests that bodily-kinaesthetic intelligence is:

- concerned with the relationship between the mental and physical, the reflective and the active

- shaped by cultural expectations.

Gardner[3] reminds us of work in Reggio Emilia when he writes:

'There are languages other than words, languages of symbols and languages of nature. There are languages of the body. These might include dance, gesture, facial expressions and so on.'

Spatial intelligence

Spatial intelligence:

- often cannot be expressed through other intelligences. While, for example, children can both draw (bodily-kinaesthetic intelligence) and talk (linguistic intelligence) about an event, thinking about space may not be so readily represented in other ways

- is concerned with the recognition and manipulation of wide space as well as more confined areas (such as jigsaw puzzles).

Musical intelligence

Gardner suggests that this intelligence:

- is the earliest to emerge
- captures the spirit of emotions
- has links to our evolution
- there are many with unusual musical talent like other intelligences, it does not stand alone. A musician needs more than musical intelligence – he or she may need spatial intelligence and bodily kinaesthetic intelligence and particularly interpersonal intelligence.

Naturalist intelligence

Gardner suggests that 'the popularity of dinosaurs among five-year-olds is no accident!' because it is an indication of our evolutionary, naturalist intelligence.[2] He goes on to identify aspects of naturalist intelligence as being seen in:

- our ability to recognise members of a group
- our phenomenal ability to identify and recognise patterns
- our propensity to categorise and classify animals, birds, insects, plants etc.

What does practice look like?

In this country, Alistair Smith has developed an approach for schools with pupils of all ages called Accelerated Learning which emphasises multiple intelligences and looks at ways, for example, of supporting bodily-kinaesthetic or spatial intelligences rather than relying on the narrowly emphasised linguistic and logical-mathematical aspects of learning.

Gardner's views appear to be constantly changing. This, together with the fact that he is quite scathing about some MIT led practice, makes it difficult to define exactly what practice would look like. In more recent times Gardner has been very admiring of practice in Reggio Emilia pre-schools. It seems likely therefore that Gardner would favour practice that include aspects of the Reggio Emilia philosophy that he admires such as:

- co-operative learning;
- artistic work;
- the involvement of parents and community; and
- discovery and debate.

Gardner considers that these six intelligences are present in each of us depending on the extent to which our background, experiences and opportunities have allowed us to develop them. He writes:[2]

> Every time we are exposed to a new individual – in person or in spirit – our own horizons broaden... Because our genes and our experiences are unique and because our brains must figure out meanings, no two selves, no two consciousnesses, no two minds are exactly alike. Each of us is therefore situated to make a unique contribution to the world.

For Gardner, creativity is not the same as intelligence. He believes that people tend to be creative only in one or two domains or areas, rather than be generally creative. He writes of Big-C creativity and assumes that this is the quality found in people like Mozart, Gandhi and Marie Curie. For him, the 'acid test' of creativity is, quite simply, has this person's work changed the nature of the subject itself?

Putting the theory into practice

There have been a number of attempts to put multiple intelligence theory into practice, particularly in Australia and the United States. At Harvard University, where Gardner works, there is a long-term project called Project Zero or Project Spectrum in which a number of academics have sought to put their theories into practice. The project is based on the assumption that 'each child exhibits a distinctive profile of different abilities, or multiple intelligences' but that 'rather than being fixed, these intelligences can be enhanced by an educational environment rich in stimulating materials and activities'.[5] You can read more about this research project in a series of books edited by Gardner, Feldman and Krechevsky.

In a comparison of Project Zero and Reggio Emilia[6] he makes the following points:

- While Project Zero began with theories, Reggio Emilia began with 'promising practices' that were developed within a theoretical superstructure.
- The emphasis in Reggio Emilia is on visual and graphic modes of representation while in Project Zero the focus is on linguistic and musical intelligences.

His influence

Multiple intelligence theory has captured popular imagination and a lot of interest is shown in finding ways to put it into practice. Gardner has prompted popular work by other academics, such as Daniel Goleman (see page 110), whose best-selling books on emotional literacy owe much to Gardner. Much of the value of his work lies in the fact that he has influenced some practitioners and policy makers to recognise the value to a broad curriculum focused on more than bare basics.

Common criticisms of his theory

There is a danger in the application of multiple intelligence theory that practitioners will trivialise the idea. Gardner claims that some schools are asking pupils whether they have exercised their intelligences today. The roots of intelligences are not always clear. For example, it is difficult to think about how personal intelligences might be subjected to a symbol system. The intelligences do not lend themselves to assessment nor are they open to testing. Gardner's selection of intelligences has also been criticised (and changed over time). In answer to this, Gardner claims that he is less concerned with which intelligences exist than the fact that everyone has a unique mix of strengths and weaknesses.

GLOSSARY

Naturalist intelligence: human understanding of the world of nature which has been limited by lack of contact with natural world.

Personal intelligences: Gardner suggests two elements – interpersonal intelligence which we use in our dealings with other people and intrapersonal intelligence which is concerned with our ability to reflect and look inward.

POINTS FOR REFLECTION

○ How do you promote co-operative learning?

○ Consider each of the six intelligences (highlighted on pages 89-90). How do you ensure that interpersonal intelligence is integrated into each of them?

○ How can you ensure that all children have opportunities to develop in all six areas?

Bodily-kinaesthetic intelligence involves action and senses

Te Whāriki

Background

Throughout the 1980s early childhood specialists and practitioners in New Zealand worked with each other and with government in efforts to develop a unified approach to early childhood care and education. It was recognised that diversity occurs in early childhood settings because of:

- Different cultural perspectives – not just the Maori and English-speaking communities, but a number of Pacific Islands that have their own language and culture.

- Differences in the pattern of attendance, full-time or part-time, daily or just one or two days a week.

- Organisational, philosophical and environmental differences: is the provision based in a home? Is the philosophical underpinning based on Montessori or Steiner? Is it described as a kindergarten, a playgroup, day nursery?

- Different local resources and levels of community involvement depending on whether the setting is in an urban or rural community; whether parents are working or not.

- Differences in the emphasis in each setting – perhaps a member of staff is particularly interested in music, or the focus is on story.

- The age range.

In a country with two dominant cultures (Maori and Western), the government was concerned to produce curriculum guidelines that could be agreed and shared by all. In 1991, Helen May and Margaret Carr won the contract to develop a curriculum. Te Whāriki (the New Zealand early years curriculum) was the result of their collaboration. A draft document was published in 1993, which was then revised and published in its final form three years later.

Underlying principles, theory or philosophy

New Zealand has had a diverse pattern of provision for early childhood care and education. Te Whāriki recognises this diversity and offers the guidance as a framework. It draws upon the philosophy of Vygotsky in particular – taking what is termed a socio-cultural approach. However, Carr acknowledges the contribution that the work of Piaget and post-Piagetians, such as Margaret Donaldson (see page 83) and Bruner (see page 63) has made. She argues that the stages that Piaget identified have 'been tipped on their side' and become 'modes of making sense of the world'[1].

The curriculum framework is rooted in an assumption that all children are 'competent and confident learners and communicators, healthy in mind, body and spirit, secure in their sense of belonging and in the knowledge that they make a valued contribution to society'. They are seen as having an abundance of skills, abilities or competencies. Whāriki is a Maori word which means 'woven mat'. The curriculum is seen as being woven from principles, aims and goals and appropriate practice – all of which are described in detail in the document.

The curriculum document states that it 'is founded on the following aspirations for children:

- to grow up as competent and confident learners and communicators;

- healthy in mind, body and spirit;

- secure in their sense of belonging; and

- in the knowledge that they make a valued contribution to society'.

It also says that provision must be based on key experiences that are appropriate to children in the following ways:

- humanly;

- nationally;

- culturally;

- developmentally;

- individually; and

- educationally.

The underlying principles are:

- empowerment;

- holistic development;

- family and community; and

- relationships.

Interwoven with the principles are the strands are well-being (including health); a sense of belonging (for children and for families); contribution (all contributions are valued and opportunities are equitable); communication (including the language and symbols of home languages); and exploration.

Putting the theory into practice

The curriculum framework was developed with the support of all sectors of early childhood care and education. The content of the curriculum is not based on traditional subject areas. It has been suggested[2] that Te Whāriki is concerned with children as they are now. It is not aimed at preparing them for the next stage of schooling. The intention is that teaching and learning should be based entirely on children's interests.

The principles are interwoven with five strands. These are:

- well-being;

- belonging;

- contribution;

- communication; and

- exploration.

Each strand is described as an aim and has three or four goals.

Shared interests of home, community and setting are promoted

For each goal there are learning outcomes – more than 100 across the five aims. There is also guidance on management and organisation of the environment for each goal, together with examples of what adults must do to support children in achieving the relevant outcomes. Examples relevant for babies, toddlers and young children are given for each goal.

The influence of Te Whāriki

Within New Zealand, the introduction of Te Whāriki has enabled many more Maori practitioners to become involved in the care and education of young children. Te Whāriki is admired in many other countries. In focusing on children's motivation to learn, it highlights the qualities or dispositions needed by learners rather than 'fragmented skills and knowledge'[5]. These include perseverance, commitment and the ability to search for learning opportunities.

Learning stories as a form of assessment has been widely adopted. They are popular with parents and practitioners and appear to have many advantages for both groups over other forms of assessment. Both find them accessible and they describe behaviour and activity which reflects the child's interests and enthusiasms. In addition[5] learning stories:

- involve children's relationships and interactions with others, which means that learning is observed within a context and not as a set of isolated skills;

- focus on what matters to the child, rather than on the demands and expectations of others;

Practitioners and parents share learning stories

- are collected in natural, rather than contrived, situations;

- pay attention to the context and the people involved in the observation;

- enable practitioners to begin with children's strengths and help them to pinpoint difficulties.

Common criticisms of Te Whāriki

Te Whāriki is widely seen as a successful approach which shows respect for children and their learning and which has sought to identify and value diversity. However, criticism to do with inclusive practice has emerged. Throughout the Te Whāriki document there is an emphasis on inclusion. Joy Cullen, a Professor of Early Education from New Zealand, has suggested[6] that despite this, many children with special educational needs in New Zealand early years settings are marginalised because they are 'Velcroed' to their support worker, and/or because they do not have strategies or opportunities to become involved with other children in their play. This criticism is not only true of Te Whāriki practice but can equally be said of the deployment of support workers in other settings and approaches.

What does practice look like?

In practice, practitioners are intended to be responsive, involved in children's play and to ask open-ended questions. Practice builds on children's interests and in order to support this, a robust system of assessment has been developed. Learning stories[3], as the assessment or observations are called, keep track of children's strengths and interests in relation to the five strands of the curriculum. Just as practitioners in Reggio Emilia believe that the learning process can be observed and recorded in their documentation, so those following Te Whāriki regard the strands of learning as being observable.

The table opposite shows the aspect that is believed to be both characteristic of and observable within each strand. Notes on each of these are recorded and together create what is called a learning story. The table also shows 'children's voice' questions which have been identified as aspects of practice which can be used to evaluate the quality of provision.

Of fundamental importance in practice, is respect for both key cultures. This has led to increased respect for cultural practice. For example, within Polynesian culture food-sharing is normal. In many nurseries this was discouraged but as practitioners reflected in practice, it was seen that such practices could be incorporated[4]. Moreover, there has been a shift away from planning based on children's individual interests towards 'shared interests in the socio-cultural contexts of home, community and centre'[4].

Although the curriculum was designed to be bicultural, MacNaughton[7] suggests that the needs and interests of some minority groups may not be represented in its approach and that it may not be possible to produce the 'one size fits all' standards which New Zealand practitioners worked hard to create.

Although the introduction and adoption of Te Whāriki throughout New Zealand has been supported through training and the publication of training resources, it has been suggested that some practitioners are too complacent about their work, using the curriculum framework to justify practices that it intended to undermine such as worksheets[5]. One of the apparent strengths of the framework has come to be seen as open to criticism. May and Carr deliberately omitted subject knowledge from the framework as they were afraid that it would result in too much emphasis on the formal aspects of learning in the early years. This has been criticised by some as failing to prepare children for school. More worryingly, it has been found that some practitioners tended to shy away from subject knowledge and that this unnecessarily limited enquiry-based learning in some cases.

Te Whāriki addresses learning from birth

POINTS FOR REFLECTION

○ Review projects or topics you have recently planned for in the curriculum. Were these based on the interests of individual children or on cultural or community interests?

○ In what ways do you and your colleagues make use of your own subject knowledge in supporting children's enquiry based learning?

○ How does your provision support children in gaining a sense of belonging and of giving?

Table showing guidance used to inform Learning Stories

Strand of Te Whāriki	Related dispositons	Observable aspect	Child's voice questions[4]	
Belonging	Courage and curiosity	Taking an interest	Do you appreciate and understand my interests and abilities and those of my family?	Do you know me?
Well-being	Trust and playfulness	Being involved	Do you meet my daily needs with care and sensitive consideration?	Can I trust you?
Exploration	Perseverance	Persisting with difficulty, challenge and uncertainty	Do you engage my mind, offer challenges and extend my world?	Do you let me fly?
Communication	Confidence	Expressing a point of view or feeling	Do you invite me to communicate and respond to my own particular efforts?	Do you hear me?
Contribution	Responsibility	Taking responsibility	Do you encourage and facilitate my endeavours to be part of the wider group?	Is this place fair for us?

Forest schools

KEY DATES

1908-1999	Gösta Frohm
1924	Chelsea Open Air Nursery School established
1995	Bridgwater College opens its forest school
2002	Creation of Forest School Initiative

LINKS

Rousseau
Pestalozzi
Froebel
Isaacs

Background

In 1995, a team from Bridgwater College, Somerset, went to Denmark on an exchange visit. They were interested in forest schools which they believed offered a unique way of building independence and self-esteem in young children. Forest schools are said to have originated in Sweden in the 1950s as a way of teaching children about the natural world. They were based on the work of Gösta Frohm, a Swede, who believed passionately in the importance of children living in and learning from nature[1].

By the 1990s, forest schools had become firmly established throughout Scandinavia. The team from Bridgwater observed children from five to seven years of age being taken to local woodland and allowed to explore the outdoor environment. They were so impressed that, on their return, they set up a forest school – the first of its kind in the UK – at the Children's Centre, Bridgwater College. This has now become a valuable model for others and the college provides training for forest school leaders and staff. In 2002, a seminar was held at Bishops Wood Centre in Worcester to assess the national interest. As a result, a Forest School England network was created with support from the Forest Education Initiative (FEI). Frohm was not an educationalist, although he became influenced by the work of Froebel. Nor was he a philosopher. Like many Swedish people, he simply believed in an entitlement of access to nature for all.

Underlying principles, theory or philosophy

The history of early childhood education is full of theorists and educationalists who placed great value on education outdoors. Almost every page of this book makes a reference to the importance of nature and fresh air, space and freedom. Friedrich Froebel talked of kindergartens – gardens of children or for children – and saw the garden as the best environment for young children's learning and development. Before then, Jean-Jacques Rousseau and Heinrich Pestalozzi, both important influences on Froebel's work, had emphasised the importance of children's interaction with nature. It should be noted that Froebel was a trained forester. Robert Owen also believed that children should spend substantial amounts of time each day outdoors.

By the beginning of the twentieth century, Margaret McMillan was trying to promote children's health, at first by establishing a night camp, where children at risk of contracting tuberculosis could sleep outdoors. The nursery school she opened in Deptford had a large garden and children were encouraged to play and rest outdoors. She later set up a large, outdoor residential camp in Wrotham, Kent so that children from Deptford could experience the countryside.

In 1916, the Order of Woodcraft Chivalry was established as an 'amalgam of religion, ritual, tradition, discipline and mystical expression, all coming together in a radical movement opposed to the given social structure'[2]. Children from four to eight years of age were known as elves. Susan Isaacs encouraged children to make good use of outdoor space in developing exploration and enquiry. In the period between the two world wars many experimental and progressive schools and movements developed. Amongst them was the Forest School that opened in the New Forest, Hampshire, in 1928, inspired by the work of the Order of Woodcraft Chivalry. It was co-educational, governed by a council of children, with gentle discipline and an informal curriculum. It emphasised the role of arts and crafts in learning.

In 1929, Chelsea Open-Air Nursery School was established. The American benefactor who established the school claimed that she was building it for 'the cripples of Chelsea', children who were so over-privileged as to be disadvantaged by not being allowed to face physical challenges and take risks. Outdoor play remains an important part of early childhood provision in the UK.

However, forest schooling claims to offer more. Despite growing enthusiasm for, and interest in it, it is quite difficult to identify the movement's aims or philosophy. A report by the New Economics Foundation suggests that the aim of such provision is to support positive attitudes to learning; offer opportunities to take risks and make choices. Forested or woodland areas are said to provide an education 'that inspires appreciation of the natural world, and, in so doing, encourage a responsible attitude to the natural world in later life'[1].

Putting the theory into practice

Sara Knight[3] suggests that a forest school can be identified by the following key elements:

- the setting is not the usual one – a place where a different set of rules can apply;

- the setting is made as safe as possible so that risky activities can be adopted – rigorous risk-assessments enable leaders to provide a safe, but not risk-free, environment;

- forest school happens over time – the recommendation is for blocks of ten weeks (with one half day each week) but a longer time is desirable. Shorter periods, such as the six weeks used in training, are often felt to end just as children's play and activity becomes richer;

- there is no such thing as bad weather, only bad clothing;

- trust is central – children need to trust adults in this new context and, in introducing activities that are not risk-free, adults need to feel certain that children will react in predictable ways;

- learning is play-based and as far as possible child-initiated and child-led;

- sessions have clear beginnings and ends;

- staff are trained.

To these characteristics, Rosaleen Joyce adds:

- ease of access to the forest school;

- familiar routines and structures in each session;

- adult enjoyment;

- involvement of parents and carers.

A safe, but not risk-free, environment is provided

What does practice look like?

This account describes practice at Bridgwater.

'The very first forest school in Bridgwater was set up in a basic and different way to the Denmark culture – small groups of six to eight children were taken onto the college sports field next to the children's centre. Gradually, the time outdoors was extended and children clearly enjoyed the freedom of being outside.

After the first successful year, plans were made to expand and develop the provision. A woodland area and a minibus were leased. The children were taken regularly to forest school sessions, accompanied by nursery nurse students, a key worker, forest school leader and a member of the children's centre management team. Each year the opportunities for the children, staff and students changed and improved. Now all the children aged three and over who attend the children's centre are given the chance to take part. All the students who will join in forest school sessions go on a compulsory three-day residential to prepare them. Before the first outing a parents' evening is held to emphasise the benefits and for parents to voice concerns. Some children are given priority of attendance – these include children with challenging behaviour or identified as having additional or specific needs. From taking part in forest school, children such as these have been observed to develop control over their behaviour, improved concentration and independence and develop their social and emotional skills. Other children, previously timid and lacking in confidence within the normal nursery environment, have become confident in their own abilities within the forest and are seen to move away from reliance on adults.

The children quickly learn the boundaries within which they must work. They respond to the sense of freedom and stick to the few rules laid down for their safety. They go out in all weathers, all year round, exploring and learning from the seasons and environment changes. Suitable clothing can be provided so that children get the most out of messy opportunities. The woodland is secure – it is in the middle of fields and entirely fenced. Because of this security, it is possible to encourage children to move away from adult interaction and become more responsible for each other and for themselves. A central camp fire and semi-permanent shelter for wood storage have been built in the woods. An old lock-up cabin acts as a secure storage unit for the tools and equipment.

At Bridgwater College Children's Centre, the curriculum of individual forest school sessions varies considerably for a number of reasons, including weather conditions, levels of staffing, group dynamics, and children's moods and interest. However, all children follow a curriculum which enables them to make as much progress as possible towards the Early Learning Goals. Every single one of the goals is worked towards throughout the year of the child attending forest school. The child's knowledge and understanding of the world, language, mathematics, creative, physical, personal and social development underpin the whole forest school philosophy.

Children are taught how to use full-size adult tools such as saws, tenon saws and pen-knives safely. They are shown how to light and deal with fires in a controlled, supervised environment. By using adult equipment, showing and preparing children, they will act in a mature and sensible way. All children's centre staff undergo some forest school training. Some may take a specific Forest School Leaders Award. In the past, children used to be able to experience a sense of freedom which then influenced their lifelong learning. At forest schools children are able to experience that now.

The influence of forest schools

The popularity of forest schools is beyond doubt.

Evaluations and anecdotes point to benefits in that there are additional staff training opportunities and increased parental involvement.

A number of positive outcomes are claimed for children in:

- Improved confidence and well-being;
- Greater independence and self-belief;
- Collaborative learning and social and emotional skills;
- Language and communication;
- Enhanced physical competence and ability to take risks safely;
- Improved physical health including reduced levels of obesity;
- The development of knowledge about the environment;
- Improved learning disposition including increased motivation and concentration;
- The development of creativity and imagination;
- Greater respect for and understanding of responsibility for our world.

Perhaps, one of the greatest influences has been recognition of the benefits of children taking risks. Woodwork, for example, was one of the traditional elements of nursery education but concerns about health and safety have seen provision all but disappear. Forest schools have had huge success in reintroducing risky activities such as the use of tools, tree climbing and fires. Moreover they have been even more successful in convincing parents of the value of such experiences.

Common criticisms of forest schools

Scandinavian research has indicated significant benefits to children but it must be remembered that there are important differences between what is offered there and provision in this country. Practice is very well-established in Scandinavia and children generally spend longer periods in the forest. The studies that have been undertaken in this country have been small-scale and have not always involved rigorous methodologies.

Some criticisms have also been made[4] of the fact that forest schools take children out of the day to day environment. It is claimed that in doing so, children are placed on the margins of society, in a kind of 'out of sight – out of mind' way. It is also suggested that while in Scandinavia forest schools are simply known as kindergartens in the usual way, the title of 'school' creates a different and unhelpful expectation in this country.

POINTS FOR REFLECTION

○ What can practitioners learn from the introduction of forest schools?

○ Should forest schools be kept as separate provision as favoured by the movement's advocates – or should the lessons learnt simply be applied to more general outdoor provision?

○ What are the benefits of offering children an environment, which, although safe, is not risk-free?

Forest school experience helps to develop positive learning dispositions

Learning through play

PROFILE

Play has been talked about and written about since time immemorial. Although practitioners in England are now required to teach through play. there is no clear consensus about what it is or how it supports learning.

KEY DATES

1917	Publication of *The Play Way* by Caldwell Cook
2012	Requirement in England to support learning through play under the revised EYFS

LINKS

Rousseau
Pestalozzi
Froebel
McMillan
Steiner
Isaacs

This section includes material written by Margaret Edgington first published in Practical Pre-School *magazine (Issue 36) as an article called 'The value of play'.*

Background

Most practitioners understand that children learn through play, but it is still consistently undervalued. Many do not understand how to support its development effectively and extend children's learning. Some are anxious about the lack of control they may have in play situations and are uncertain about how to manage a playful environment. Others do not feel able to articulate the arguments which support play as a means of learning or do not feel confident about planning for play in ways which meet the demands of heads and Ofsted inspectors. Research[1] found that few early years practitioners could explain why play is an important vehicle for learning.

But this is not new. Even before the nineteenth century, Rousseau had been arguing for children's freedom. Froebel developed ideas of play but his gifts and occupations would look very different from the free-flow play advocated in the twenty first century by Froebelian Tina Bruce. In 1917, Caldwell Cook published a book entitled *The Play Way* in which he declared that his heart was set on a course of action which would ensure that play-based approaches to education would permeate all schools, including secondary schools. Sadly his dream has not yet come true.

For the first time in this country, the revised Early Years Foundation Stage (EYFS), published in 2012, requires practitioners to reflect three characteristics of children's learning in their teaching. The first of these is playing and exploring – which involves finding out; using play symbolically in role play and in pretending that objects are something other than they are. It also involves initiating new ideas, seeking challenge, taking risks and learning from failures. These ideas are not new and are reflected in curricula in Reggio Emilia, New Zealand's Te Whāriki and in Steiner Waldorf practice around the world. However they do signal that play is important in children's learning.

Underlying principles, theory or philosophy

Perhaps, one of the reasons why practitioners appear confused about play is that there is a confusing array of theories and explanations for it. Unable to identify one clear definition, it has been suggested that theories may be categorized as follows[2]:

- romantic theories – the child is considered as a whole; play is part of children's nature and children are happy when playing and learning. This view is linked to Rousseau's and to Froebel's theories;

- behaviourist theories – linked to Skinner's theory. It suggests that after learning, children deserve to play. Play is used as a reward;

- therapeutic theories – as in the psychoanalytical theories of Freud and others, children are seen as struggling with fears. Play helps children to deal with fears and anxieties but it can also help them to learn to empathise with others. This can help children to develop awareness of how others feel and how to manage their own emotions. Winnicott argued that play was essential to creativity, while fellow psychoanalytical theorist Melanie Klein saw play as a therapy in its own right. Susan Isaacs' practice was rooted in the idea that children use play to deal with fears and anxieties;

- cognitive theories – more recent theories of play, including those based on neuroscience and current developmental psychology, emphasise its contribution to the development of problem solving, creativity, communication and developing understanding of social rules. These ideas are most firmly linked to Piaget and Vygotsky. Isaacs also made rich provision for exploratory play as she understood the value of play in helping children to make sense of their world;

- biological theories – scientists and psychologists are coming to the view that since playfulness is present in all humans it must have a biological function. It has been suggested that play supports the development of creativity and imagination which is essential to the development of the flexible and adaptable human brain;

economic theories – it has been suggested that in the face of all these arguments, the most cost effective and efficient approach to teaching and learning will include play.

It is clear that there can be no simple definition of play. However there is some agreement about what it involves that may help to define play[3]. Play is likely to be open-ended, self-chosen and self-directed. It will probably be enjoyable and satisfying but is not always fun – as when children persist with gritted teeth to get something right. Jennie Lindon[4] defines play as 'a range of activities, undertaken for their own interest, enjoyment or the satisfaction that results'. This is a useful working definition which incorporates the characteristics identified in this paragraph.

Tina Bruce writes about children 'wallowing in free-flow play' and argues that play serves the function of co-ordinating learning. Players may operate in a group or alone but contact with others is essential to play and learning, since it makes the learner take account of other people's ideas and feelings

It is sometimes suggested that 'Children do not make a distinction between "play" and "work" and neither should practitioners.' Froebel famously suggested that play is the child's work while for Montessori practitioners work and play are the same thing – engendering 'freedom of choice, the exercise of will and deep engagement which leads to concentration'[5]. However we should not forget that for children, play is something they choose to do while work is something they are required to do.

Putting the theory into practice

Children must feel motivated and in control of their play. If an adult starts to take over, it stops feeling like play to children. Play must be open-ended. There should be no required outcome for everyone to achieve. Instead, each child should be able to explore in their own way, and come to their own conclusions or achieve their own goals.

In play, children draw on and develop their past experiences and are prompted by their interaction with materials and other people to explore new knowledge, language and skills. Children's play always has a purpose for the child. The child who seems to be aimlessly pouring water may be practising a newly gained skill, may be reliving the experience of

Play and exploration requires unscheduled time

Time is needed to make friends and play with ideas and materials

seeing a waterfall or may be feeling anxious or sad and gaining comfort from this calming activity. He or she may be exploring a particular schema (see page 6-7) or may be engaged in scientific enquiry.

However, the purpose may not be readily apparent to adults. It is this lack of certainty about play, and that it cannot be controlled, which worries many parents and practitioners. The learning that takes place during or as a result of play can often not be seen. Parents may put pressure on practitioners to get their children to produce work on paper because they think that this is evidence of learning. A knowledgeable practitioner is able to expose the limitations of paper-based exercises for young children. By sharing their observations of children's play and explaining to parents what they show about children's thinking and learning, parents can be led to a better understanding of the value of play. For example, children show much more sophisticated levels of understanding of number and quantity in role play when calculating what is needed for a picnic than they do when poring over a worksheet. In play, children see the point of what they are doing and thinking about, stretching themselves to the limit of their abilities. This is often not the case when they are asked to complete an adult-directed task.

Why is play important for early learning?

It can be helpful to be clear about why play is so important to learning and development. Arguments for play include the fact that:

- all of us learn best when we want to do something and are least likely to learn when we are being made to do something that doesn't interest us. Children are naturally drawn to play experiences and concentrate for long periods in their self-chosen play. Play offers children the chance to be in control, and to feel competent, within relevant, meaningful and open-ended experiences, for example reading and writing with a real purpose and without fear of getting it wrong (such as spontaneously taking a message when on the telephone in role play or taking on a powerful role, such as the mum or the doctor);

- in their play, children are able to meet their own needs and to make sense of their own often confusing world. Play involves exploring feelings, ideas, materials, relationships and roles, making connections between one experience and another and representing ideas, objects and environments;

opportunities within play to use one thing to represent another (for example a block as a mobile phone) lay important foundations for the later use of abstract symbols, such as letters and numbers, to represent ideas. As they get older, children begin to develop longer, more complex story lines in their play. This is a vital foundation for writing.

In a study comparing children who had been taught to read at an early stage and those who had not been introduced formally to reading until they were seven years old, Suggate suggests that the vital components of successful reader in the long-term are play, language and interaction with adults[6].

- play encourages creativity and imagination. It is intellectually, socially, emotionally, physically and linguistically challenging and encourages children to work in depth (alone and with others). It can offer all children the chance to explore and learn at their own pace and stage of development. It has a crucial role in enabling children to consolidate learning, particularly at a time when the pace is too fast for some children'

- imaginative play supports the development of abstract thinking which is of particular importance in mathematical development;

- play is important because it enables adults to observe children at their highest level of competence and to see their ideas, concerns and interests. Lev Vygotsky (see pages 51-54) said that in their play, children are 'a head taller than themselves'. Early years practitioners who take time to observe their children at play will know exactly what he meant.

The influence of play

Early years practitioners who have been convinced of the power of play for a very long time will recognise the importance of a requirement in England to teach through play. This is a major breakthrough. At the end of the foundation stage, practitioners must comment on the ways in which children have developed skill as a player and how this has contributed to their learning and development. Suggate's study of reading also highlights the broad influence of play in the early years.

It should also be remembered that play and creativity are closely linked. Currently, neuroscience is highlighting the link but several decades ago Winnicott was able to say that it is only in play that children and adults become creative. This echoes the views of many artists, including Picasso, who highlight the link between child-like behaviour and creativity. It is interesting to note that many countries such as Singapore, where children apparently do well in formal situations, are reviewing their curricula to see how they can help children to be more creative.

Play therapy continues to be of value to troubled children. It provides a means for them to express and explore events or experiences which they cannot easily put into words.

What does practice look like?

When adults argue that 'we didn't play when we were at school and it didn't do us any harm' they are forgetting that they had rich opportunities to learn through play at home and in their community. If children growing up today do not experience a substantial amount of play in an early years setting, they will be missing out on many of the character building and life-enhancing experiences many of us took for granted.

Conditions under which most children today are growing up makes it vital to provide rich and extended play experiences. In today's society they have:

- much less freedom to play out of doors;

- less opportunity to socialise and play with other children away from an adult;

- less opportunity for play in mixed age groups – not only is there less street play but most children come from smaller families;

- more visual input from television, computers, videos and pictures in books, together with fewer opportunities to listen and create mental images.

Teachers and other practitioners interpret children's need to play in different ways. For some, relying on outmoded behaviourist theories, play can simply mean going to the home corner for ten minutes after the child has completed their work. For others it might involve playing a maths board game – playful learning but not play. Since real play involves choice and freedom we must build that into the curriculum. Ten minutes is not long enough to develop meaningful play. Research shows that children making a later start to formal schooling generally achieve more academically because their early years experience was meaningful and gave them a more solid foundation for later learning.

As Margaret McMillan's words remind us, children need time and space in which to flourish. For what Tina Bruce calls 'free-flow play' the following are essential:

- an environment which offers open-ended resources; natural materials, sufficient space in which to move around (indoors and out);

- extended periods of time in which children can develop play;

- an emotional climate which encourages involvement, supports play and helps children to manage conflict;

- adults who support and scaffold learning and who value, encourage and extend children's chosen play.

Common criticisms of play

Despite the wealth of evidence which exists about how children learn, there are still people who continue to believe that formal education – sitting and listening – supports learning. We now know a great deal about dispositions for learning and how readily the urge to learn and develop with which children are born can be damaged. Practitioners have a responsibility to help parents and others who do not understand its value, to a better understanding of learning.

Play can be messy, noisy and difficult to manage. This requires skill and patience. Practitioners who value play and what it offers for children must work to ensure that it is safeguarded. Similarly, some people resist providing opportunities for play because they believe it to be dangerous. In undertaking risk assessments, it is vital to assess what children will lose if they do not undertake particular activities or experiences.

Since we now know that learning to manage risk is a vital part of creativity and learning, we must ensure that, as in forest schools (see page 96), we create sufficiently safe environments that are not entirely without challenge.

Some criticism of play comes from postmodern thinkers. Such theorists seek to challenge all assumptions and to see things from a variety of perspectives. Throughout this section there is an assumption that play is important. Postmodernists argue that not all parents share that view, that in poverty stricken countries play is a luxury that cannot be afforded; or even that some sections of Western society require more control than a play-based curriculum offers.

These are difficult arguments but it is worth spending some time thinking them through. More information on the importance given internationally to children's right to play can be found on pages 118-119.

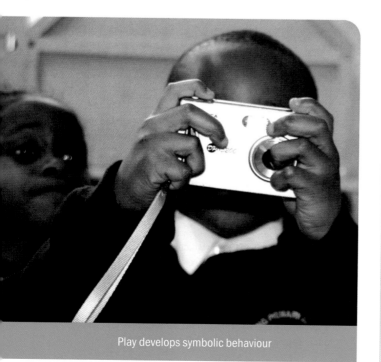

Play develops symbolic behaviour

POINTS FOR REFLECTION

○ Observe a child engaged in play. Think about whether they are playing alone or in a group, whether the activity was self-chosen and if it is open-ended.

○ Observe a child who seems difficult to engage. Try to observe him or her is a situation which is adult-directed and one which is self-chosen. Are there any indications of how he or she might be helped to be more autonomous?

○ How can you ensure that children have sufficient space for high quality play?

How children learn

Research into brain development

PROFILE

Emerging evidence about how the young child's brain develops has focused on the importance of providing the best possible learning environment during the early years. Here are some of the findings of current research and their implications for early care and education.

Based on material written by Dr Jillian Rodd first published in Practical Pre-School magazine (Issue 29).

Background

The brain and its relationship with the mind has excited scientific interest over centuries. In earlier times it was only possible to study the brains of the dead or of animals. However techniques now available, such as brain imaging, have given scientists the opportunity to look in more detail at what is going on inside our heads. However we should be mindful of Cohen's warning that 'the more we know about the brain, the more we realise how little we know about how our ability to think develops'[1].

Neuroscience, in a similar way to genetics, is often seen as holding the answer to all the questions we have about the brain – but we should remember too that not all neuroscientists hold the key to understanding. Not all neuroscientists are psychologists, nor are all developmental psychologists neuroscientists. Insights from both studies of the brain and of behaviour can support one another in aiding our understanding.

The brain is often likened to a computer or even the internet or a browser but it is important to realise that throughout history scientists have come up with metaphors for the brain – devices to help them imagine how the brain works. Before his death in 1650, French philosopher René Descartes described the brain as a hydraulic machine – the most advanced technology of his day. Freud thought of the emotions building up in the brain as like pressure building up in a steam engine. Similarly it has been likened to a telephone switchboard or an electrical circuit.

A child's brain begins to develop before it is even born. A developing foetus has its full complement of about 100 billion neurons and the first connections between neurons are already formed. After birth, the process accelerates rapidly with the brain quadrupling in volume by

Physical activity is vital to brain development

adulthood. This extra volume is made up of new synapses or connections between cells and it is these that are critical for learning and memory.

Space does not allow for a full account of current understandings of the brain. Even if it did, before long, the information would be likely to be out of date since new knowledge or theories emerge constantly. It is wise to be cautious about what you read and hear – for as we will see there is a great deal of misinformation about the brain.

Underlying principles, theory or philosophy

Current theories suggest that the neuronal connections present at birth are laid down, sculpted and reinforced by regular use. If they are not activated, they decay or are pruned. This process allows those connections which are used frequently more space to grow, explaining young children's obvious 'hunger for experiences' or drive to learn. Infants play an active role in shaping their own brain.

Humans learn through imitation

For example, vision is one of the new-born's primary sources of information but the least mature of the senses. During the first six months, the visual cortex, which controls the sending and receiving of visual information, continues to develop until the infant's vision is as clear as an adult's.

Babies actively seek out faces in preference to other patterns within half an hour after birth. This speeds up the development of brain connections that process this type of recognition information, so that the baby can quickly distinguish between mum, who represents food, security and comfort – and a stranger. Babies are particularly attuned to the sound of the human voice. Talking softly and singing to a baby helps develop connections in its brain. The developing brain of young children benefits from the rich and stimulating experiences gained through normal, everyday interactions with caring people.

Development of the brain begins in the foetus and continues until death. However, a timetable controls the brain's natural maturation, making specific physical and mental activities from conception to about 15 months. It ensures that basic survival needs, such as food, shelter, security and safety, are met. It also controls sensory and motor development, which means that young babies' brains require daily opportunities for sensory activation and motor exploration.

From 15 months until about four and a half years of age, the limbic system (see page 109) becomes active, providing the young child with the growing capacity to understand self and others, emotions and language. However, from birth babies are able to imitate others. They will imitate facial expressions such as poking the tongue out. This has been attributed to mirror neurons in the brain, sometimes called empathy neurons. The theory is that imitating others enables babies' to come to know how others feel.

From about four to seven years, the right hemisphere of the brain makes further expansion of cognitive, language, emotional and physical skills possible. However, it is not until approximately seven to nine years of age, with further development of the left hemisphere, that the capacity for reading and writing increases. This suggests that early formal academic learning experiences are inappropriate because children's brains generally do not have the capacity to master such skills until about seven years of age. There is increasing evidence to support this view (see example of Steiner influence on page 37).

Myths about the brain

Some of the misinformation about the brain has become firmly fixed in the popular mind as fact. Listed below are a few of the myths that surround thinking about the brain.

1. It is not true that the brain is like a computer. Although it is useful to think about it in this way the description does not do justice to the human qualities, feelings and foibles that operate within the brain.

2. It is not true that left and right brains operate in isolation. In almost all cases the two sides of the brain operate in harmony – although it is true that they have different functions. Language, for example, is controlled from many different areas of the brain. Mathematics is popularly thought of as a logical activity controlled by the left side of the brain (in most people). However research shows that mathematically gifted students were more likely than others to integrate thinking from both sides of the brain in solving maths problems[2].

3. It is not true that we use only 10% of our brains or that we have 100 billion brain cells. We appear to have around 86 billion brain cells. There is some evidence that cells in the area of the hippocampus – the centre of the limbic system – can regenerate supporting memory. Any mentally complex activity uses many different areas of the brain, so that over of the course a day, just about all of the brain is engaged. This is underlined by the fact that damage to even a small area of the brain can have serious repercussions.

4. It is not true that all brain damage is irreversible. Especially in young babies and children, the brain is described as plastic – meaning that it is able to take on the role of damaged areas. Human brains are flexible – a fact that accounts for our creativity. Animals that rely on reflex action are less able to change behaviour whereas humans' long childhood allows for play and exploration, which shape the brain in individual ways.

5. It is a myth that listening to Mozart makes you more intelligent. Music is helpful in many ways. Some studies show that it can increase performance on a limited range of tasks. There is also some evidence that learning an instrument improves concentration, self-confidence and coordination. However there is no evidence for what has been termed the Mozart effect – nor that listening to the music of any other composer actually increases intelligence. It may improve mood.

Putting the theory into practice

Factors that promote brain development

The brain's ability to 'wire' itself depends on a child's exposure to simple learning experiences, such as making sense of faces and patterns and being involved in conversations. Even seemingly mundane experiences, such as staring at toys hanging over a cot or dropping toys and watching them being picked up contribute to this process. Babies' brains focus their mechanisms for recognising speech at an early age. An infant's repeated exposure to words and vocal interaction clearly helps the brain build neuronal connections that will enable language to be learned later on.

It appears that there are critical periods or windows of opportunity during which the brain is honing particular skills or functions, for example, binocular vision (seeing with both eyes) and language development, specifically the ability to grasp grammatical rules. If the chance to practise a skill is missed during its particular window, the child may be disadvantaged.

Factors that hinder brain development

Considerable evidence suggests that poor pre- and post-natal environments, inadequate nutrition, inappropriate diet, insufficient water and lack of oxygen impede brain growth and reduce the capacity for sensing, learning, thinking and acting. Young children's brain development appears to be particularly sensitive to stress. Stress raises the level of the steroid hormone cortisol that can destroy brain cells and the neural connections needed for later learning. This hormone can trigger hyperactivity, anxiety and impulsive behaviour. It can result in dissociative behaviour where the child switches off and appears uncommunicative.

Chronic stressful experiences, particularly before the age of three when the brain is at its most malleable, can hypersensitise children to stressful events which can diminish their ability to concentrate, form relationships and function normally. When children operate in a state of chronic stress, changes to the structure of the brain seem to occur. It is essential that stress be minimised wherever possible for young children.

Understanding of the brain has developed alongside technology

What does practice look like?

Neuroscience is very popular and practitioners are often keen to take advantage of new findings. Some secondary schools are considering, for example, starting their classes later in the morning in line with American research suggesting that teenagers do not like early starts – not because they are inherently lazy, but because they have a natural sleep pattern that leads to a late-to-bed, late-to-rise cycle.

In fact, classroom interventions based on rigorous scientific evidence are surprisingly scarce. Guy Claxton[3] warns against 'brain-friendly learning'. We assume that water can only be beneficial – but Claxton cites evidence that drinking water when you are not thirsty hinders learning. Many practitioners are keen on the idea of "learning styles" but in fact, as we have seen, all areas of the brain need to be engaged for successful learning. Telling someone that they are a kinaesthetic learner will not improve their learning. The available tests are inadequate and poorly researched. Moreover, particularly in the case of young children, we should be developing all channels of learning rather than the ones we think may be preferred. All young children should be learning through physical and tactile action. All should be learning to listen closely and observe well.

Care and attention

The work which has been collated from neuroscientists, researchers and early childhood practitioners indicates that one of the best ways to promote brain development in young children is through responsive care from loving parents and adults. Adult attention is vital because it helps give meaning and context to the developing structures in the brain, thereby grounding learning in social experience. Stimulating the developing brain's potential does not mean that adults need to resort to specialised or high technology. Many adults provide appropriate, responsive care in their day-to-day interactions with young children.

However, a growing body of research indicates that brain growth and development is nurtured by careful attention to all aspects of the child's development – physical, social, emotional, language and cognitive. The infant is born with a pre-disposition to learn and will seek out appropriate stimulation when it is required. Adults need to respond sensitively to children's communications about their learning needs.

Children living in environments that are deprived of stimulation, talk, play and love grow up in unfavourable circumstances. Those who are not played with, sung to, talked to, who receive little tactile stimulation from adults and those who have suffered stressful and traumatic experiences may end up with brains that are measurably smaller or structurally less complex than healthy, loved children.

Many neuroscientists not previously concerned with education, have offered evidence which supports child-centred practices. Ramachandran[4] suggests, for example, that creativity and humour should be part of the curriculum since they involve making unusual connections in the brain. Susan Greenfield[5] states that 'play is fun with serious consequences'.

The main lessons from brain studies for early childhood practitioners suggest that:

- good pre- and post-natal care is vital;

- warm and loving attachments between young children and adults are essential; positive, age appropriate stimulation from birth enhances children's development and learning for a lifetime;

- second language learning is easier in the early years;

- the presence of mirror neurons suggests that imitation is of vital importance in learning;

- learning is enhanced when the left and right hemispheres are encouraged to work together. This can be done through activities such as music and dance;

- encouraging visualisation can enhance language development. This may include the use of sign, gesture and facial expression;

- early intervention works best from the first weeks of life;

- inter-professional work involving neuroscientists, early childhood education practitioners and developmental psychologists is important to a good understanding of learning and development.

Downshifting to a psycho-physiological response occurs when a child is confronted with cognitive tasks that are inappropriate, meaningless, repetitive or present a threat of failure. Environments and teaching strategies that impose undue stress, boredom or fatigue cause some learners to downshift, thereby impeding brain growth and affecting the brain's ability to function at high levels. Early exposure to formal, prescriptive and academic learning experiences can lead to downshifting, thus explaining the disaffection with and disengagement from learning evident in some young children.

The influence of research into brain development

It would be difficult to overestimate the extent to which neuroscientific study engages practitioners. Claxton argues that non-specialist practitioners do not have enough time or knowledge to scrutinise findings into brain research that are presented to them. Worryingly, it appears that non-specialists are 'more likely to believe a bad explanation for something if it contains references to neuroscience'[3].

Work on the brain and physicality has probably influenced the decision to make physical development a prime area of learning in the revised EYFS in England. Neuroscientist Susan Greenfield has, for example, highlighted the relationship between the brain and physical action suggesting that if we didn't move we wouldn't need a brain[5]. Sally Goddard Blythe, a neuro-physiological psychologist, has written extensively[6] about the need for reflex actions to be inhibited in order to make way for higher order thinking and action. For example, the Moro reflex normally disappears by the age of four months. If it does not it can lead, she argues, to impulsive behaviour which disrupts learning.

The excitement that is characteristic of young children is important for learning. When excited, the chemistry of the brain changes, making learning more effective. This, and other similar findings, should influence practitioners to welcome excitement. Of course, in large groups, the excitement must be managed and channelled but it remains important for development.

Common criticisms of research into brain development

While emerging information about how the young child's brain develops is exciting and illuminating, it is also essential that it is correctly interpreted and translated appropriately into effective early care and educational practices. We now know that young minds can do more at an earlier age than was previously assumed and that stimulating experiences in natural settings are necessary.

However, prescribing experiences or formal scripts for social or cognitive interactions must be avoided because this results in children's achievements being evaluated too narrowly. Rigid assumptions about what children can, should and will be able to do are not helpful. Unrealistic expectations about the progress of any child, including those with special needs, should be avoided. Narrowing the focus of learning and ignoring the holistic nature of development is detrimental to the well-being of young children.

John Bruer challenges the idea the widely-held view that the first three years of life are of particular importance. He argues that children of all ages have particular needs and that very young children ought not to be privileged[7]. Young brains are flexible and many children are sufficiently resilient to withstand difficulties in their lives. However, it is more economical (and kinder) to prevent emotional damage to young children than to try and put it right at a later stage.

MacNaughton[8] argues that although practitioners are often keen to legitimise their practice by reference to scientific data, they must take on neuroscientific findings with caution. Findings are likely to change in the light of subsequent research. Moreover, the children and families with whom we work are diverse and unique – there are no simple, single answers.

The brain thrives on interaction

GLOSSARY

Limbic system: a group of interconnected deep brain structures involved in emotion, motivation, and behaviour.

Mirror neurons: a mirror neuron is a neuron that fires both when an animal acts and when the animal observes the same action performed by another.

Hemispheres: the brain is made up of left and right halves, or hemispheres.

Hippocampus: a part of the brain that is involved in emotions, learning and memory formation.

Moro reflex: a normal reflex of young infants; a sudden loud noise causes the child to stretch out the arms and flex the legs.

POINTS FOR REFLECTION

○ Review your understanding of learning styles. What can you do to ensure that all the children with whom you work have opportunities to develop a range of learning styles?

○ What do you think children gain from imitating others and how can you support it?

○ Look for examples of young children's humour. Why might this be helpful to brain development?

Emotional intelligence

PROFILE

'Emotional intelligence' is a phrase made popular by psychologist and author Daniel Goleman. Goleman defines emotional intelligence as: knowing one's feelings and using them to make good decisions in life; being able to manage moods and control impulses; being motivated and effectively overcoming setbacks in working towards goals.

KEY DATES

1969	*Freedom to Learn* by Carl Rogers is published
1976	Ferre Laevers begins work on experiential education
1983	*Frames of Mind* by Howard Gardner is published
1996	*Emotional Intelligence* by Daniel Goleman is published
1998	*The Emotional Brain* by Joseph LeDoux is published

LINKS

Gardner
Freud
Research into brain development
Isaacs

Based on material written by Caroline McAdam first published in Practical Pre-School *magazine (Issue 28).*

Background

An approach designed to bridge psychoanalytic theory and behaviourism was developed in the1940s by Carl Rogers, Charlotte Buhler and Abraham Maslow. They termed their approach humanistic psychology and it was designed to tackle:

- the denial of emotions and feelings underpinning behaviourism;

- the lack of respect given to clients by psychoanalysts, who, for example, described patients as hysterics.

Gradually Rogers' approach to therapy came to be seen as having application for education and in 1969 he published a book entitled *Freedom to Learn*. He emphasises trust and excitement and suggests that the role of child-initiated learning is supporting interest, involvement and understanding.

In the 1970s, a Belgian, Ferre Laevers, began to study 'deep-level learning' – work which was to lead to the development of scales for measuring children's emotional well-being and levels of involvement in their learning. The two scales have become highly influential in early education – providing one answer to the criticism that assessment in education too often measures things that may be easy to measure but unimportant, while ignoring things that are important but difficult to measure.

In 1983, Howard Gardner published the first edition of *Frames of Mind*. His theory of multiple intelligences[1], outlined in that book included two personal intelligences – interpersonal intelligence and intrapersonal intelligence. The first relates to the ability to interact effectively with others, the second focuses on the ability to reflect on self. Daniel Goleman borrowed Gardner's powerful use of the word 'intelligence' and developed the concept of emotional intelligence.

Underlying principles, theory or philosophy

Emotional intelligence is defined as the capacity to acquire and apply information of an emotional nature, to feel and respond emotionally. It means being able to understand what others are feeling, managing emotions in relation to others and being able to persuade and lead others. Emotional competencies are skills and attributes such as self-awareness, empathy, impulse control, listening, decision-making and anger management. Emotional literacy is the term used to describe the ability to experience and manage emotions productively.

Goleman has been highly successful in capturing the public imagination in his choice of phrase but that is not to denigrate his achievement. While his work is written in a popular style it is underpinned by serious research. Academics such as Joseph LeDoux, neuroscientists such as Susan Greenfield and developmental psychologists such as Colwyn Trevarthen all underline the vital importance of emotions to learning and development. In turn, their work is underpinned by the pioneers of early education such as McMillan, Isaacs and Steiner who understood that children's emotions controlled their ability to learn and flourish.

The power of emotions

Experts in brain development know that emotions are the ignition switch for learning for all of us. As we learn more about the brain and how it develops we understand that the emotional mind can and often does over-ride the rational mind. There are three distinctive parts to the brain: the reptile brain, the limbic system and the neo-cortex. The reptilian brain is the most primitive part of the brain. It regulates basic life functions like breathing, monitors motor functions, controls reactions, movement and behaviours that are repetitive, predictable and rarely constructive. The reptilian brain is designed to keep the body running and ensure survival. It is responsible for our 'fight or flight' response when we are faced with danger or negative stress.

As the brain evolved new layers were added. The new layers surrounded the brainstem or reptilian brain like a ring and are called the limbic system. The new neural territory added powerful emotions to the brain's repertoire. When we are in the grip of anger, full of dread or head over heels in love, the limbic system has us in its grip. This system filters valuable data in and useless data out. It governs our concept of value and truth and is the site of long-term memory and goal setting.

The neo-cortex has evolved most recently and is the seat of thought. It contains the centres that put together and comprehend what the senses perceive. It is responsible for our ability to solve problems, discern relationships and patterns of meaning and it generates meaning from sensory data all of the time.

A small structure in the limbic region of the brain, the amygdala, is the centre of the emotional mind. It scans every incident for trouble. It charges into action without considering the consequences and in moments of crisis or intense passion the emotional brain dominates. This affects the behaviour of very young children but again in adolescence may make it difficult for teenagers to control their actions.

Putting the theory into practice

Emotions play a critical part in teaching and learning. We therefore need to make sure that early years settings are emotionally positive and supportive workplaces for all learners. If learners are exposed to emotionally negative stressors then the reptilian brain dominates and the fight or flight response locks in. No learning takes place. Survival is the key objective. This means that we need to create an environment that:

- is safe and secure;

- is rich in sensory stimuli;

- is able to meet the needs of learners;

- is empowering, supporting decision-making and making choices;

- is conducive to positive relationships;

- is free from negative stressors, such as hunger, thirst, threat;

Emotional security is key to learning and development

What does practice look like?

Goleman identifies four building blocks for incorporating emotional intelligence in educational settings:

- safety, security, unconditional love and nurturing; at no stage of development is this of greater importance than in the early years. Gerhardt[2] echoing Bowlby's work reminds us that the extent to which babies and young children feel loved and valued determines the extent to which they are sufficiently well-balanced emotionally to make a full contribution to the society in which they are growing up. In essence, early childhood practitioners have to place emotional security at the heart of all they do.

The role of the key person is vital in establishing security – a familiar person who knows the child's routines and foibles, can talk confidently to parents or other significant carers, in whom the child can trust.

- stimulating environments; babies and young children do not benefit from hot-housing but they do gain from being in an environment that allows space, time and freedom alongside clear and loving expectations. They need stimulation indoors and out – novel enough to be stimulating, but familiar enough to feel secure.

- experimental learning opportunities to engage skills, knowledge and attitudes in a wide variety of real-life tests; play and exploration with opportunities for challenge and open-ended solutions.

- useful and timely performance feedback – it is not helpful to over-praise children but they should be given clear feedback on things done well. Simply saying well done is not enough – but adding what you particularly like about something a child has done or the way in which they have done it, allows the child to reproduce the same thing later. This will mean saying things like "Well done – you really concentrated while you were painting" or "That structure you've made out of boxes is amazing. It's very tall but you've also managed to stop it wobbling."

It is also important to make feedback positive – try to avoid mentioning the negatives. So instead of saying "don't throw balls where there are people" you can highlight preferred positive actions "great! You managed to get the ball into that box – even though it's so far away." Young children benefit from feedback when this is given immediately.

The role of parents

It would be wrong to leave this section without mentioning parents. Family life is a child's first school of emotional learning. Within the family unit they learn how to feel about themselves, how others will react to those feelings, how to think about these feelings and the choices they have in reacting. Children learn to express themselves, to read others and handle their feelings through modelling or mirroring the significant adults in their lives. The approaches and responses of people around them profoundly influence the children's developing sense of emotions and their impact on daily life.

When parents or other significant people respect children, children learn to respect themselves and each other. Children's confidence and independence depend on their ability to see themselves as reasonably competent and responsible. Adults therefore need to give children real responsibilities through which they can learn. Some parents may need the support of practitioners in achieving this. As Julia Manning-Morton reminds us[3], adults (including practitioners) are often unaware of the way in which children's emotions chime with or trigger ours. It's important to look carefully at why we as adults react strongly in some situations.

- is emotionally positive, so that feelings are recognised, understood and dealt with effectively;

- fosters achievement and celebrates success;

- is respectful of the difference between learners;

- promotes self-esteem.

It is important not to neglect the emotional life of young children. Feelings, self-awareness, life skills, conflict management and self-esteem are critically important. Emotions direct our behaviour, shape our values and predispose us to choose one course of action over another. They drive us to action, push or pull us away from certain people, objects, actions and ideas. Emotions allow us to defend ourselves in dangerous situations, to love, grieve and protect the things we value.

How children function each day and throughout life is determined by both rational intelligence and emotional intelligence. When the two perform together smoothly and efficiently, a child develops in emotional intelligence and intellectual ability. There is evidence to suggest that those who are emotionally literate are at an advantage in life. Learning involves developing our feelings along with our ability to think and act. How we do in life is determined by our emotional as well as our rational skills.

Most learning involves other people. Working and learning together, discussing our ideas and understandings with others, helps us to develop our personal skills. It also enables us to express a range of emotions, to develop them and to learn to use them effectively. It is, therefore, important to create a stimulating environment where there are plenty of opportunities to make choices and decisions about the learning that is taking place. Adopting an approach which assumes that young learners are capable of managing themselves, their relationships and their own learning puts the child at the centre of the learning process. Engaging children's minds in investigating aspects of their own experiences and environments helps them to develop a deeper sense of competence and self-worth.

To be most effective, emotional literacy content and processes should be applied consistently across the curriculum. Children need many opportunities for practice. When emotional lessons are repeated over and over, they become positive habits that surface in times of stress. By suggesting relationships and posing the right questions, by being observant and noticing non-verbal signals, adults can help to highlight and deal with emotional aspects of everyday learning. More importantly, they can take moments of personal crisis and turn them into lessons in emotional competence.

The influence of theories of emotional intelligence

The importance of young children's emotional well-being has long been a concern of early childhood practitioners. Over the past forty years, society in general has come to recognise its importance to all of us. Although rooted in psychoanalytic theory, it has taken the popularisation of the idea – triggered initially by Gardner's interpersonal and intrapersonal intelligence and latterly by Goleman's clever use of a phrase which captures the public imagination.

In almost all walks of life the importance of emotional intelligence and well-being is acknowledged, if not always wholly acted upon. But in the early years it has been reinforced by the work of development psychologists such as Colwyn Trevarthen. His role in framing curriculum guidance for children up to three in Scotland, together with work on the role of key persons and the identification of personal, social and emotional development as a prime area of learning in England's revised EYFS, reflect steadily growing influence.

Ferre Laevers work has also influenced practitioners and policy makers. His scales for well-being and involvement have encouraged practitioners to engage more fully in how children are learning and given policy makers clearer insight into the vital importance of what can be seen as soft measures.

Common criticisms of theories of emotional intelligence

Criticisms are most likely to come from people who regard learning as something passive and formal – rather than involving action and excitement. Those who favour rote learning are unlikely to see the value of an approach which places feelings and emotions at the heart of education.

It is also possible to criticise a focus on emotional well-being on the grounds that feelings which practitioners cannot manage may be unleashed. In Laevers' screening for well-being, for example, attention may be drawn to unhappiness which goes beyond the classroom or setting. In this case it is vital that practitioners know which professionals they can call on and how to access their services.

Family life is the first school of emotional learning

GLOSSARY

Amygdala: a structure in the limbic system that is linked to emotions and aggression.

POINTS FOR REFLECTION

○ Observe a colleague. Does he or she offer children positive and timely feedback?

○ Does your environment offer sufficient challenge and novelty for all children?

○ Does your key person system offer sufficient security for all children? Are there ways in which it could be improved?

Introduction

1. Gardner (1996) *Intelligence: Multiple Perspectives*, Rinehart and Winston, Holt (page 97).

John Comenius   (1592-1670)

References

1. www.comeniusfoundation.org/comenius.htm
2. Comenius, J. (1896) *The Great Didactic,* Adam and Charles Black, London (first published in 1657).
3. Cited in Nutbrown et al. (2008) *Early Childhood Education*, Sage, London.
4. Piaget, J. (1957) 'Jan Amos Comenius (1592-1670)' in *Prospects* vol. XXIII no.1/2 1993 pp173-196, Unesco International Bureau of Education (http://www.ibe.unesco.org/publications/ThinkersPdf/comeniuse.PDF).

Where to find out more

- www.comeniusfoundation.org
- Pound, L. (2013) *Quick Guides for early development: physical development*, Hodder, London (see Chapter 8).

Jean-Jacques Rousseau   (1712-1778)

References

1. Rousseau, J-J. (1974) *Emile*, Dent and Sons (comments are in the introduction to this edition of *Emile*, which was written by P.D. Jimack).
2. Nutbrown et al. (2008) *Early Childhood Education*, Sage, London.

Where to find out more

- Wokler, R. (2001) *Rousseau: A Very Short Introduction*, Oxford University Press.
- The Rousseau Association (www.rousseauassociation.org).

Johann Heinrich Pestalozzi   (1746-1827)

References

1. Green, J. A. and Collie, F. A. (1916) *Pestalozzi's Educational Writings*, Edward Arnold (quote from page 1).
2. Pound, L. (2011) *Influencing Early Childhood Education*, Open University Press, Maidenhead (see page 3).
3. Joyce, R. (2012) *Outdoor learning: past and present*, Open University Press, Maidenhead (see Chapter 4).
4. Mayer, F. (1960) *A History of Educational Thought* (2nd ed), Charles Merrill Books Inc., Columbus OH.

Where to find out more

- Joyce, R. (2012) *Outdoor learning: past and present*, Open University Press, Maidenhead (see Chapter 4).
- For more information about the Pestalozzi Children's Villages, visit the website: www.pestalozziworld.com

Robert Owen   (1771-1858)

References

1. Donnachie, I. (2000) *Robert Owen: Owen of New Lanark and New Harmony*, Tuckwell Press.
2. Whitbread, N. (1972) *The Evolution of the Nursery-Infant School*, Routledge and Kegan Paul. (Whitbread cites Owen on page 14)
3. Nutbrown et al. (2008) *Early Childhood Education*, Sage, London.
4. van der Eyken (1967) *The Pre-School Years*, Penguin Books, Harmondsworth.

Where to find out more

- Donnachie, I. (2000) *Robert Owen: Owen of New Lanark and New Harmony*, Tuckwell Press.
- Pound, L. (2011) *Influencing early childhood education*, Open University Press, Maidenhead (see Chapter 1).
- http://robert-owen-museum.org.uk

Friedrich Froebel   (1782-1852)

References

1. Bruce, T. (1987) *Early Childhood Education*, Hodder and Stoughton (Bruce cites Froebel on page 11. The reference is to Froebel's book *The Education of Man*, published in 1887).
2. Singer, E. (1992) *Childcare and the Psychology of Development*, Routledge (Singer cites Froebel on page 52).
3. Blackstone, T. A. (1971) *Fair Start: the Provision of Pre-school Education,* Allen Lane.
4. Aspin, D. N. 'Friedrich Froebel: visionary, prophet and healer?' *Early Childhood Development and Care* Vol 12 (1983).
5. Read, J. 'A Short History of Children's Building Blocks' in Gura, P. (ed) (1992) *Exploring Learning,* Paul Chapman Publishing (Jane Read describes the Gifts on page 5).

Where to find out more

- http://www.froebeltoday.com (for examples of gifts and occupations).
- Joyce, R. (2012) *Outdoor learning: past and present*, Open University Press, Maidenhead (see Chapter 5).

Sigmund Freud   (1856-1939)
and psychoanalytic theories

References

1. (2001) *Complete Psychological Works of Sigmund Freud*, Vintage Press, London.
2. Manning-Morton, J. and Thorp, M. (2003) *Key Times for Play*, Open University Press.
3. Manning-Morton, J. (2011) 'Not just the tip of the Iceberg: psychoanalytic ideas and early years practice' in Miller, L. and Pound, L. (eds) *Theories and Approaches to learning in the early years*, Sage, London.
4. MacNaughton, G. (2003) *Shaping Early Childhood*, Open University Press).

Where to find out more
- www.freud.org.uk
- www.psychematters.com/bibliographies

John Dewey   (1859-1952)

References
1. Mooney, C. G. (2000) *Theories of Childhood: an Introduction to Dewey, Montessori, Erikson, Piaget and Vygotsky*, Redleaf Press.
2. Pollard, A. (2002) *Readings for Reflective Teaching*, Continuum.

Where to find out more
- Mooney C. G. (2000) *Theories of Childhood: an Introduction to Dewey, Montessori, Erikson, Piaget and Vygotsky*, Redleaf Press.
- http://infed.org/mobi/john-dewey-on-education-experience-and-community/

Margaret McMillan   (1860-1931)

References
1. Whitbread N. (1972) *The Evolution of the Nursery-Infant School*, Routledge and Kegan Paul.
2. McMillan M. (1919) *The Nursery School* (first published in 1919 by Dent and revised in 1930).

Where to find out more
- Pound, L. (2011) *Influencing Early Childhood*, Open University Press.
- Lowndes G. (1960) *Margaret McMillan, The Children's Champion*, Museum Press.

Rudolf Steiner   (1861-1925)
and Steiner Waldorf education

References
1. Nichol, J. (2007) *Bringing the Steiner Waldorf Approach to your Early Years Practice*, David Fulton, London.
2. Drummond, M-J., Lally, M. and Pugh, G. (eds) (1989) *Working with children: developing a curriculum for the early years*, National Children's Bureau (the quote comes from page 59).
3. Steiner Waldorf Education (2009) *Guide to the Early Years Foundation Stage in Steiner Waldorf Early Childhood Settings*, The Association of Steiner Waldorf Schools, Forest Row.
4. Howard Gardner in his book *The Unschooled Mind* (Fontana Press, 1991) states that it is no accident that in most societies children do not begin statutory schooling until the age of six or seven, since it is only at that stage that they can usefully deal with symbol systems such as print.
5. Suggate, S. (2009) School entry age and reading achievement in the 2006 programme for International Student Assessment (PISA) *International Journal of Education Research* 48:151-161.
6. Pound, L. (2011)) *Influencing early childhood education: key figures, philosophies and ideas*, Open University Press, Maidenhead.
7. Drummond, M-J. (1999) 'Another way of seeing: perceptions of play in a Steiner kindergarten' in Abbott, L. and Moylett, H. (eds) *Early Education Transformed*, Falmer Press, London.

Where to find out more
- Heckman, H. (2008) *Childhood's Garden Spring Valley*, WECAN Books, NY (this book includes a DVD which illustrates many aspects of practice).
- House, R. (ed) (2011) *Too much too soon*, Hawthorn Press.
- Nichol, J. (2007) *Bringing the Steiner Waldorf Approach to your Early Years Practice*, David Fulton, London.
- Parker-Rees, R. (ed) (2011) *Meeting the Child in Steiner Kindergartens*, Routledge, London.
- Pound, L. (2011) *Influencing early childhood education: key figures, philosophies and ideas*, Open University Press, Maidenhead (see Chapter 4).
- Taplin, J. (2011) 'Steiner Waldorf Early Education: offering a curriculum for the 21st century' in Miller, L. and Pound, L. (eds) *Theories and Approaches to Learning in the Early Years*, Sage Publications, London.
- International Association for Steiner Waldorf Education (www.iaswece.org).
- www.steinerwaldorf.org.uk (these sites include DVD material giving information about Steiner Waldorf education in this country and abroad).
- http://openeyecampaign.wordpress.com (this site gives access to Open Eye Newsletters, which have video footage and updates on Steiner Waldorf early years education).
- www.eurythmy.org.uk
- www.otago.ac.nz/news/news/otago006408.html (for information on research into a later introduction to formal reading instruction (Accessed 18/10/11)).

Maria Montessori   (1870-1952)
and the Montessori method

References
1. MacNaughton, G. Shaping Early Childhood (Open University Press, 2003) citing Montessori.
2. Montessori, M. (1948) *From Childhood to adolescence*, New York: Schocken Press.
3. Bradley, M. et al. (2011) 'Maria Montessori in the United Kingdom: 100 years on' in Miller, L. and Pound, L. (eds) *Theories and Approaches to learning in the early years*, London: Sage.
4. Smith, L. *To Understand and to Help* (Associated University Presses, 1985).

Where to find out more
- http://www.montessori.org.uk/__data/assets/pdf_file/0009/99882/Manifesto_40pp_LR.pdf
- Bradley, M. et al. (2011) 'Maria Montessori in the United Kingdom: 100 years on' in Miller, L. and Pound, L. (eds) *Theories and Approaches to learning in the early years*, Sage, London.

Susan Isaacs   (1885-1948)

References
1. Isaacs, S. (1929) *The Nursery Years*, Routledge and Kegan Paul.
2. Smith, L. (1985) *To Understand and to Help: the Life and Works of Susan Isaacs*, Fairleigh Dickinson University Press.
3. van der Eyken, W. and Turner, B. (1975) *Adventures in Education*, Pelican Books.
4. Drummond, M-J. (2010) Editorial *Early Education* 61 Summer.

Where to find out more
- Graham, P. (2009) *Susan Isaacs: a life freeing the minds of children*, Karnac Books, London.

Jean Piaget   (1896-1980)

References
1. Donaldson, M (1978) *Children's Minds* (Fontana) (Both quotes are taken from the website www.time.com/time/time100/scientist/profile/piaget.html).
3. Gopnik et al (1999) *How Babies Think*, Weidenfeld and Nicolson.

Where to find out more
- Athey, C. (2007) *Extending Thought in Young Children*, Paul Chapman Publishing.
- Cohen, D. (2002) *How the Child's Mind Develops*, Routledge (see Chapter 2)
- Pound, L. (2011) *Influencing Early Childhood Education*, Open University Press (see Chapter 12).

Lev Vygotsky   (1896-1934)

References
1. Gray, C. and MacBlain, S. (2012) *Learning theories in childhood*, Sage, London.
2. Bruner, J. (1986) *Actual Minds Possible Worlds*, Harvard University Press, London.
3. Rogoff, B. (2002) *Learning together: children and adults in a school community*, Oxford University Press, Oxford.
4. Rogoff, B. (2003) *The Cultural Nature of Human Development*, Oxford University Press.

Where to find out more
- Pound, L. (2011) *Influencing early childhood*, Open University Press, Maidenhead (see Chapter 13).
- Rogoff, B. (2002) *Learning together: children and adults in a school community*, Oxford University Press, Oxford.

Burrhus Skinner   (1904-1990)
and behaviourist theories

References
1. Slater, L. (2004) *Opening Skinner's Box*, Bloomsbury, London.
2. Keenan, T. (2002) *An Introduction to Child Development*, Sage.
3. MacNaughton, G. (2003) *Shaping Early Childhood*, Open University Press.
4. Kohn, A. (1993) *Punished by Rewards*, Houghton Mifflin.

Where to find out more
- Palmer, J. (2001) *Fifty Modern Thinkers on Education*, Routledge.
- Slater, L. (2004) *Opening Skinner's box*, Bloomsbury.
- http://www.nobelprize.org/educational/medicine/pavlov/readmore.html

John Bowlby   (1907-1990)

References
1. Gerhardt, S. (2004) *Why love matters*, Brunner/Routledge, Hove.
2. Siegel, D. (1999) *The Developing Mind*, Guilford Press, New York.
3. Singer, E. 'Shared care for children' in Woodhead, M. et al. (1998) *Cultural Worlds of Early Childhood*, Routledge in conjunction with the Open University.

Where to find out more
- Pound, L. (2011) *Influencing Early Childhood Education*, Open University Press, Maidenhead (see Chapter 9).
- http://eyfs.info/articles/_/child-development/attachment-theory-and-the-key-person-approach-r64

Jerome Bruner   (1915-)

References
1. Gardner, H. 'Jerome S Bruner' in Palmer, J. (ed) (2001) *Fifty Modern Thinkers on Education*, Routledge.
2. Bruner, J. (1960) *The Process of Education*, Harvard University Press.
3. Bruner, J. (1996) *Culture of Education*, Harvard University Press.
4. Bruce, T. (2011) *Early Childhood Education* (4th ed), Hodder.
5. Bruner, J. (1980) *Under Five in Britain*, Grant McIntyre, London.

Where to find out more
- www.infed.org/thinkers/bruner.htm
- Smidt, S. (2011) *Introducing Bruner*, Routledge, London.

Chris Athey   (1924-2011)
and schema theory

References
1. Athey, C. (1990) *Extending Thought in Young Children*, Paul Chapman Publishing.

How children learn

2. Bruce, T. (2011) *Early Childhood Education*, Hodder.
3. http://juliangrenier.blogspot.co.uk/2009/11/schema-theory-in-early-years-education.html
4. http://juliangrenier.blogspot.co.uk/2010/12/researching-early-childhood-pedagogy.html#more

Where to find out more
- http://juliangrenier.blogspot.co.uk/2009/11/schema-theory-in-early-years-education.html
- Bruce, T. (2011) *Early Childhood Education* (4th ed), Hodder.
- Matthews, J. (2003) *Drawing and Painting: Children and Visual Representation*, Paul Chapman Publishing.
- Meade, A. and Cubey, P. (2008) *Thinking Children*, Open University Press.
- Nutbrown, C. (2011) *Threads of Thinking* (4th ed), Paul Chapman Publishing.
- Arnold, C. (2010) *Understanding Schemas and Emotion in Early Childhood*, Sage.

Loris Malaguzzi (1920-1994)
and early education in Reggio Emilia

References
1. Malaguzzi, L. 'History, ideas and basic philosophy' in Edwards, C. et al. (eds) (1993) *The Hundred Languages of Children – the Reggio Emilia approach to early education*, Ablex.
2. Malaguzzi et al. (1995) *A journey into the rights of the child*, Reggio Children.
3. www.sightlines-initiative.com
4. Giudici et al. (2001) *Making Learning Visible*, Project Zero/Reggio Children.
5. Moss, P. 'The otherness of Reggio' in Abbott, L. abd Nutbrown, C. (eds) (2001) *Experiencing Reggio Emilia*, Open University Press.
6. Browne, N. (2004) *Gender Equity in the Early Years*, Open University Press.

Where to find out more
- Edwards, C. et al. (2012) *The Hundred Languages of Children – the Reggio Emilia Approach to Early Education*, Praeger.
- www.sightlines-initiative.com
- http://www.reggiochildren.it/?lang=en
- The municipality has an organisation which publishes and distributes a range of books, pamphlets and videos. Full details can be found on both the Reggio Children and Sightlines-Initiative websites above.

Paulo Freire (1921-1997)

References
1. Taken from Fromm's book *The Heart of Man* (page 234).
2. MacNaughton, G. (2003) *Shaping Early Childhood*, Open University Press.

Where to find out more
- www.infed.org/thinkers/et-freir.htm

David Weikart (1931-2003)
and the HighScope approach

References
1. MacNaughton, G. (2003) *Shaping Early Childhood*, Open University Press.
2. Epstein et al. (2011) 'The HighScope Approach' in Miller, L. and Pound, L. (eds) *Theories and Approaches to learning in the early years*, Sage, London.

Where to find out more
- Epstein et al. (2011) 'The HighScope Approach' in Miller, L. and Pound, L. (eds) *Theories and Approaches to learning in the early years*, Sage, London.
- www.highscope.org

Margaret Donaldson (1926-)
and post-Piagetian theories

References
1. Hughes, M. 'Margaret Donaldson' in Palmer, J. A. (ed) (2001) *Fifty Modern Thinkers on Education*, Routledge.
2. Donaldson, M. (1978) *Children's Minds*, Fontana.
3. Worthington, M. and Carruthers, E. (2003) *Children's Mathematics*, Paul Chapman Publishing, London.
4. Carr, M. (2001) *Assessment in early childhood settings: learning stories*, Paul Chapman Publishing, London.

Where to find out more
- Donaldson, M.(1978) *Children's Minds* by Margaret, Fontana.
- 'Margaret Donaldson' in Palmer J. A. (2001) *Fifty Modern Thinkers on Education*, Routledge (pages 175-181).

Howard Gardner (1943-)
and multiple intelligence theory

References
1. Gardner H. (1989) *To Open Minds*, Basic Books Inc.
2. Gardner H. (1999) *Intelligence Reframed*, Basic Books Inc.
3. Gardner, H. (1993) *Frames of Mind* (2nd ed), Fontana.
4. Krechevsky, M. and Seidel, S. 'Minds at work: applying multiple intelligences in the classroom' in Collins, J. and Cook, D. (eds) (2001) *Understanding Learning: Influences and Outcomes*, Paul Chapman Publishing in association with The Open University.
5. Chen at al. (1998) *Building on Children's Strengths: the experience of Project Spectrum*, Teachers' College Press.

6. Giudici, C. et al. (2001) *Making learning Visible: Reggio Project Zero and Reggio Children* (page 338).

Where to find out more
- Smith, A. (1996) *Accelerated Learning*, Network Educational Press.
- Krechevsky, M. and Seidel, S. 'Minds at work: applying multiple intelligences in the classroom' in Collins, J., Cook, D. (eds) (2001) *Understanding Learning: influences and outcomes*, Paul Chapman Publishing/The Open University.

Te Whāriki

References
1. Carr, M. (2001) *Assessment in early childhood settings: learning stories*, Paul Chapman Publishing London.
2. Fleer et al. 'A Framework for conceptualising early childhood education' in Anning, A., Cullen, J. and Fleer, M. (eds) (2004) *Early Childhood Education: society and culture*, Sage Publications.
3. Carr, M. (1998) *Assessing Children's Learning in Early Childhood Settings*, New Zealand Council for Educational Research.
4. Ritchie, J. (2005) 'Implementing Te Whārikias postmodern practice: a perspective from Aotearoa/New Zealand' in Ryan, S. and Grieshaber, S. (eds) *Practical transformations and transformational practices: globalization, postmodernism and early childhood education*, Elsevier Ltd, Kidlington, Oxford.
5. Smith, A. (2011) 'Relationships with people, places and things – Te Whāriki' in Miller, L. and Pound, L. (eds) *Theories and Approaches to learning in the early years*.
6. Cullen, J. 'Adults co-constructing professional knowledge' in Anning, A., Cullen, J. and Fleer, M. (eds) (2004) *Early Childhood Education: society and culture*, Sage Publications.
7. MacNaughton G. (2003) *Shaping early childhood*, Open University Press, Maidenhead.

Where to find out more
- (1996) *Te Whāriki: Developmentally Appropriate Programmes in Early Childhood Services*, New Zealand Ministry of Education, Learning Media.
- Smith, A. (2011) 'Relationships with people, places and things – Te Whāriki' in Miller, L. and Pound, L. (eds) *Theories and Approaches to learning in the early years*.

Forest school

References
1. Joyce, R. (2012) *Outdoor learning: past and present*, Open University Press.
2. Selleck, R. J. W. (1972) *English Primary Education and the Progressives 1914-1939*, Routledge and Kegan Paul (see page 38).
3. Knight, S. (2013) *Forest School and Outdoor Learning in the Early Years* (2nd ed), Sage.
4. Tovey, H. (2007) *Playing outdoors: spaces and places, risk and challenge*, Open University Press.

Where to find out more
- http://www.forestschools.com/case-studies/early-years-and-pre-school/
- http://www.forestry.gov.uk/pdf/SERG_Forest_School_research_summary.pdf/$FILE/SERG_Forest_School_research_summary.pdf
- Knight, S. (2013) *Forest School and Outdoor Learning in the Early Years* (2nd ed), Sage.
- Joyce, R. (2012) *Outdoor learning: past and present*, Open University Press.
- Blackwell, S. and Pound, L. 'Forest schools in the early years' in Miller, L. and Pound, L. (eds) (2011) *Theories and approaches to learning in the early years*. Sage.

Learning through play

References
1. Moyles, J., Adams, S. and Musgrove, A. (2002) *Study of Pedagogical Effectiveness in Early Learning Research Report No 363*, Department for Education and Skills.
2. Guha, M. 'Play in school' in Blenkin, G. and Kelly, A.V. (eds) (1987) *Early Childhood Education*, Paul Chapman Publishing.
3. Hughes, F. (2003) 'Spontaneous play in the 21st century' in O. Saracho & B. Spodek (Eds.), *Contemporary perspectives on play in early childhood education* (pp. 21-40), Information Age Publishing, Greenwich, CT.
4. Lindon, J. (2001) *Understanding Children's Play*, Nelson Thornes.
5. Montessori Schools Association/DCSF (2008) *Guide to the Early Years Foundation Stage in Montessori Setting*, Montessori St. Nicholas/DCSF, London.
6   Suggate, S. (2009) School entry age and reading achievement in the 2006 programme for international student assessment (PISA). *International Journal of Education Research* 48: 151-6.
7. The Convention on the Rights of the Child was adopted by the General Assembly of the United Nations, 20 November 1989.

Where to find out more
- Bruce, T. (2001) *Helping Young Children to Play*, Hodder and Stoughton.
- Jenkinson, S. (2001) *The Genius of Play*, Hawthorn Press.

International Association for the Child's Right to Play

What is play?
- Children are the foundation of the world's future.

- Children have played at all times throughout history and in all cultures.

- Play, along with the basic needs of nutrition, health, shelter and education is vital to develop the potential of all children.

- Play is communication and expression, combining thought and action; it gives satisfaction and a feeling of achievement.

- Play is instinctive, voluntary and spontaneous.

- Play helps children develop physically, mentally, emotionally and socially.

- Play is a means of learning to live, not a mere passing of time.

Article 31 of the Convention on the Rights of the Child[7] states that:

Parties recognise the right of the child to rest and leisure, to engage in play and recreational activities appropriate to the age of the child and to participate freely in cultural life and the arts.
Parties shall respect and promote the right of the child to participate fully in cultural and artistic life and shall encourage the provision of appropriate and equal opportunities for cultural, artistic, recreational and leisure activity.

Research into brain development

References
1. Cohen, D. (2002) *How the child's mind develops*, Routledge, London.
2. http://www.apa.org/pubs/journals/releases/neu-182371.pdf
3. Claxton, G. (2008) *What's the point of school?* One World, Oxford.
4. Ramachandran, V. S. and Blakeslee, S. (1999) *Phantoms in the Brain*, Fourth Estate.
5. Greenfield, S. (1996) *The Human Mind Explained,* Marshall.
6. Goddard Blythe, S. (2005) *The well balanced child*, Hawthorn Press, Stroud, Gloucs.
7. Bruer, J. (1999) *The Myth of the first three years*, The Free Press.
8. MacNaughton, G. (2004) The politics of logic in early childhood research: a case of the brain, hard facts, trees and rhizomes. *The Australian Educational Researcher 31*, 3 December.

Where to find out more
- Goddard Blythe, S. (2005) *The well balanced child*, Hawthorn Press, Stroud, Gloucs.
- Blakemore, S-J. and Frith, U. (2005) *The Learning Brain: lessons for education*, Blackwell Publishing, Oxford.

Emotional intelligence

References
1. Gardner, H. (1983) *Frames of Mind*, Fontana.
2. Gerhardt, S. (2004) *Why love matters: how affections shapes a baby's brain*, Brunner-Routledge, Hove.
3. Manning-Morton, J. (2011) 'Not just the tip of the iceberg: psychoanalytic ideas and early years practice' in Miller, L. and Pound, L. (eds) *Theories and approaches to learning in the early years*, Sage, London.

Where to find out more
- Goleman, D. (1996) *Emotional Intelligence*, Bloomsbury.
- Manning-Morton, J. (2014) *Exploring well-being in the early years*, Open University Press.

Index

Index

W

....

X

....

Y

....

Z

....

Thanks to Angela Shaw, my tireless publisher, for putting so much time and energy into this book.

Thanks too to Chris, who supports and encourages me in every possible way.

Photo credits

Every effort has been made to locate copyright owners of the images used in this book. Permission to use photographic images was given by the individuals and institutions listed below. Omissions brought to our attention will be corrected. For permission to reproduce these images please contact the owners.

All inner photos © MA Education Ltd and taken by Lucie Carlier, with the exception of the following:

Page 4: © Bettmann/CORBIS

Page 6: © Bettmann/CORBIS

Page 9 (Theorist picture): © Mary Evans Picture Library – INTERFOTO/ Sammlung Rauch

Page 13: © Mary Evans Picture Library

Page 17 (Theorist picture): © Mary Evans Picture Library

Page 21 (Theorist picture): © Hulton-Deutsch Collection/CORBIS

Page 22: photo taken by Ben Suri

Page 27 (Theorist picture): © CORBIS

Page 30: photo taken by Ben Suri

Page 31 (Theorist picture): © Mary Evans Picture Library

Page 34: © Mary Evans Picture Library

Page 38: © Mary Evans Picture Library

Page 46: © Mary Evans Picture Library/Epic

Page 51 (Theorist picture): © UIG via Getty Images

Page 55 (Theorist picture): © Mary Evans Picture Library/Epic; main image photo taken by Ben Suri

Page 63: © Archives of the History of American Psychology, The Center for the History of Psychology, The University of Akron

Page 67 (Theorist picture): By kind permission of the family

Page 71: © Preschools and Infant-toddler Centers – Istituzione of the Municipality of Reggio Emilia from the Catalogue of the Exhibition "The Hundred Languages of Children", Reggio Children publisher, 1996

Page 82: photo taken by Ben Suri

Page 87 (Theorist picture): © J.L. CEREIJIDO/epa/Corbis

Page 107: Photo: © JON WILSON/SCIENCE PHOTO LIBRARY